MOON MOUNTAIN

Bibhutibhushan Bandopadhyay (born 1894) was a distinguished Bengali novelist and writer. His literary career began in 1921 with the publication of his first short story *Upekshita* in *Probashi*, a prominent Bengali literary magazine of the day. In 1928, the epic *Pather Panchali* was published and Bibhutibhushan achieved instant celebrity in popular as well as critical circles, becoming a household name in the world of Bengali culture and letters. *Pather Panchali* and its sequel *Aparajito* were later celebrated in Satyajit Ray's unforgettable cinematic rendition of the 'Apu' trilogy. His other major works, encompassing an impressive range of genres and themes, include *Aranyak*, *Icchamoti*, *Adarsha Hindu Hotel*, *Heera Manik Jwale*, *Maraner Danka Baje*, *Debjan*, *Jatrabadol* and *Dristi Pradeep*.

Pradeep Sinha was born on August 28, 1942. He graduated with honours in Economics from St. Xavier's College, Calcutta, and worked in several firms as a marketing executive before joining Orient Longman in 1987. *Moon Mountain*, his translation of Bibhutibhushan Bandopadhyay's *Chander Pahar*, was his first literary project. He died on 2 February 2001.

Moon Mountain

Bibhutibhushan Bandyopadhyay

Orient BlackSwan

ORIENT BLACKSWAN PRIVATE LIMITED

Registered office
3-6-752, Himayatnagar, Hyderabad 500 029 (A.P), INDIA
e-mail: centraloffice@orientblackswan.com

Other offices
Bangalore / Bhopal / Bhubaneswar / Chennai / Ernakulam / Guwahati
Hyderabad / Jaipur / Kolkata / Lucknow / Mumbai / New Delhi / Patna

First published by Orient Longman Private Limited 2007
First edition 2007
First Orient Blackswan impression 2011

Cover and book design

ISBN: 978 81 250 3069 0

Typeset in AdobeGaramond 13/16.8 by
OSDATA, Hyderabad

Printed in India at
Graphica Printers
Hyderabad 500 013

Published by
Orient Blackswan Private Limited
3.6-752, Himayatnagar, Hyderabad 500 029 (A.P), India
e-mail: hyderabad@orientblackswan.com

Contents

Introduction

Bibhutibhushan's literary output was astonishingly varied in scope and subject. Even leaving aside his two hundred and odd short stories and considering only his novels, it is surprising and also somewhat humbling to learn that the author of the largely autobiographical *Pather Panchali* and *Aparajita* is the same person who wrote the introspective *Aranyak* and the philosophical fantasy *Debjan*. Or that the gourmet and master of culinary intricacies who authored *Adarsha Hindu Hotel* seems also to have travelled widely in the wildest regions of Asia and Africa, and produced remarkably detailed, concrete narratives from the lived experience, in the form of adventure stories for young people.

Yet, in a sense, *Chander Pahar* closely resembles *Pather Panchali* in spirit. In spite of the vast differences in narrative pace and setting, both books draw on the same yearning for the unknown, a passion for adventure and for lands beyond the horizon. Young Apu often sat at the window during the lazy afternoon hours, staring at the high-flying kites circling like specks around the golden minarets of the clouds, until the lonely splendour of the scene sometimes made him weep silently, he knew not why. He would fetch his elder sister and show her the distant sky. "How very far, isn't it? How very far!"[1] But this charm of the remote was lost on Durga. "Crazy boy," she would say affectionately. "Crazy boy, showing me how very far!"

This is the very passion which fuels Apu's imagination all his life and, in *Aparajita*, takes him to Fiji. It also informs the celebrated ending of *Pather Panchali*, where the god of roads and ways speaks to Apu about unending travel. And it is the same passion which inspires Bibhutibhushan to write *Chander Pahar*.

When the novel begins, Europe's late nineteenth-century 'scramble for Africa' was only in the recent past; it was the age in which Queen Victoria's government bid to eliminate French and German competition on African territory by establishing direct imperial rule over regions it had previously controlled only through military and economic means and, above all, to acquire hidden repositories of fabled resources. Mungo Park, Henry Morton Stanley, David Livingstone, Richard Burton and others who led the push into the 'dark continent' became heroic figures and their travels were the stuff of legend.

---

[1] All translations used in this introduction, except those in the excerpts from *Moon Mountain*, are mine. For *Moon Mountain*, I have used Mr Pradeep Sinha's work.

Bibhutibhushan was ten years old when Stanley died in 1904. Burton had been gone for less than fifty years and Sven Hedin, who explored vast regions of Central Asia, was only just past his prime when *Chander Pahar* was conceived in the late 1930s. The book resonates with a pioneer's thrill and exaltation at moving deeper and deeper into an unknown and dangerous country, of facing and surviving its strange perils.

Unlike the great explorers he admired, however, Bibhutibhushan never set foot outside British India. He was a great traveller, but mainly on foot. To the west his peregrinations did not extend much beyond Varanasi and, to the east, they were limited to certain parts of the Indian north-east and present-day Bangladesh. This is all the more remarkable in view of the absolute ease and mastery with which he wields a wealth of authentic zoological, botanical, geological, astronomical and meteorological information which forms the backbone of the plots in his adventure stories. It is a testimony to his narrative craft that this information never interferes with the plot or reads like a high school lesson, but invariably becomes integral to the story being told. Consider this, for example:

A branch line was being built from the main track, connecting Mombasa with Kisumu on Lake Victoria, and Nyanza. The place was 350 miles west of Mombasa and seventy-two miles south-west of Knudsburg station of the

Uganda Railways. Shankar had come there as a clerk and store-keeper in the construction camp. He lived in a small tent. There were a number of other tents around his—no houses had yet been built—arranged in a circle in a large clearing. All around them were stretches of open land, full of tall grass interspersed with a few trees or shrubs. On the outer edge of the tents, where the grassland came to an end, was the famous tree of Africa, the baobab.

A detailed account of Shankar's brief sojourn in the savannah follows, featuring encounters with man-eating lions, the infamous Black Mamba and other deadly snakes, cavalier Portuguese cardsharps and many such perils. This part, especially the description of the line-laying work and the problem with the lions, draws heavily on the personal experiences of John Henry Patterson, soldier and author, who was commissioned by the British East Africa Company in 1898 to supervise the construction of a railway line in Kenya. There were a number of Indian menials working in his team, and Patterson's brave conduct in dealing with the notorious twin man-eating lions that plagued the Tsavo area earned him a written felicitation from his workers—penned by one Baboo Purshotam Hurjee Purmar, Overseer and Clerk of Works—in January 1899. These incidents are chronicled in his popular book *The Man-Eaters of Tsavo* (1907). Bibhutibhushan owned a copy, which still features in his personal library that has been inherited by my father.

However, sources become more and more difficult to identify as Shankar and Diego Alvarez penetrate the inner depths of the virgin wilderness. Rich details are strewn like small gems casually along the way, much like the perfect tetrahedron diamond crystals Shankar will find in the labyrinth. Alvarez works in an orange plantation for a few months after returning from his expedition with Jim Carter. Shankar reads a five-day-old edition of the *Kenya Morning News* by firelight, sitting outside his tent in Uganda. The Englishman of Tabara asks them to travel carefully during the day so as to avoid the bite of the tsetse fly, which induces the sleeping sickness. They board a steamer at Port Uzizi to cross Lake Tanganyika, then buy resources at Albertville and proceed to Kabalo by Belgian rail, thence to undertake a three-day journey to Sanikini, across the Congo river.

Little touches like these fill out a plot already rich in detail with flesh and marrow, rendering the story absolutely credible and giving it the concreteness of actual lived experience. To paraphrase what Keats once said to Shelley in the course of their famous correspondence, Bibhutibhushan 'loads every rift with rich ore'. Each paragraph contains some intimate reference to the ground realities of everyday life in the African outdoors, creating a background as finely textured and interconnected as the intricately criss-crossed network of liana creepers in the heights of the Richtersveld rainforests, until the reader has no choice but to suspend disbelief.

In his brief foreword to *Chander Pahar*, Bibhutibhushan cites the writings of the explorers Rosita Forbes and Harry Hamilton Johnston (not to be confused with Harry Frederick Johnston, Surveyor General of Western Australia from 1896 to 1915) as his main sources for the story. But Forbes' travels were restricted to Libya, Ethiopia and Yemen, and Johnston, though widely travelled in Africa, was primarily a statesman and administrator, and only incidentally a botanist and explorer. Surely, the rich setting of *Chander Pahar* was not derived from these sources alone. Rather, the reader senses the existence of a vast hinterland of background learning, perfectly absorbed so that it could be drawn upon without unwieldiness and internalised so completely that the author himself might be hard pressed to remember what he owed to whom.

One of Bibhutibhushan's main sources was certainly the *Wide World Magazine* (founded by George Newnes in 1898, and issued till 1965)—a monthly publication containing adventure stories for the Edwardian gentleman and bearing the motto 'Truth is Stranger than Fiction'. In spite of getting involved in a couple of hoaxes, *Wide World Magazine* continued to enjoy a certain prestige, and even earned the distinction of being recommended as reading for young boys by H.G. Wells in his book *Mankind in the Making* (1903). Newnes was also the publisher of the famous *Strand Magazine*, in which Conan Doyle's Sherlock Holmes stories first appeared. Bibhutibhushan was a regular subscriber to *Wide World Magazine*, and received issues by airmail from London for several years. We still preserve in our home ancient bound volumes of entire years' issues, some bearing Bibhutibhushan's signature.

My father remembers reading in his youth, in one of these volumes (now lost), a tale of two young men on a promotional campaign for the Enfield Cycle Company who undertook to ride their Royal Enfield motorcycles across Death Valley in California without stopping to service or repair any part of their vehicles. Upon their successful completion of the feat, *Wide World Magazine* bought exclusive rights to their story, which contained (says my father) an incident very similar to the *Chander Pahar* episode in which Shankar finds the skeletal remains of Attileo Gatti and a rotting keg of brackish, inky water in a kopje on the outskirts of the Kalahari desert.

Incidentally, Attileo Gatti was a real-life adventurer and amateur film maker who led several expeditions (sponsored by Hallicrafters Company of Chicago, an electronic equipments manufacturer) to the Rwenzori mountains of Uganda in the second quarter of the twentieth century. This range was known in ancient times as the Mountains of the Moon, first named thus by the Greek merchant-traveller Diogenes and later popularised by the geographer and mathematician Ptolemy. Bibhutibhushan derives the title of *Chander Pahar* thence.

The apocrypha surrounding Gatti's expeditions contain references to a certain anthropoid ape, larger than even the gorilla and far more ferocious, living among the rainforests of the Rwenzori range. This monster was called *mulahu* by the local Mambuti pygmies, who were terrified of it. No white man had seen it yet, and finding it was one of the alleged objectives of a Gatti expedition. All this sounds very like the *Bunip* of *Chander Pahar*, except that *bunyip* is the native name of yet another fabled monster of uncertain appearance and with a fearsome cry, belonging not to Africa but to Australian aboriginal mythology and believed to be a denizen of creeks, swamps and billabongs. *Dingonek*, yet another name used in the story for the monstrous guardian of the Richtersveld diamond mines, can be traced to the folklore of West African tribes of the Congo river-basin, and bears little resemblance to the anthropoid ape with three-toed feet which caused the deaths of Jim Carter and Diego Alvarez. It seems that Bibhutibhushan took a few liberties with his cryptozoology!

Not being a bona fide expert on the subject, Bibhutibhushan also makes at least one mistake in his zoology—he has wolves in Africa, but there are none in the entire continent except a very rare and diminutive sub-species that is found in the far north of Egypt. The frightened cub that takes refuge in Shankar's tent during the volcanic eruption is identified as a wolf. Shankar is surrounded at night by concentric circles of coyotes and wolves on the Chimanimani mountains. Some editors and translators have taken pains in the past to substitute these references with something more 'correct', but it is perhaps best to leave a text as it was written, with all its errors and discrepancies, for the sake of retaining its authentic flavour.

I am happy that Mr Pradeep Sinha did exactly that. He has succeeded in preserving the spirit and charm of the Bangla story while remaining faithful to the literal meaning and plot sequence—a daunting task. I hope readers shall find his work interesting enough to be motivated to read *Chander Pahar* in the original. However, the English text is a story in its own right and stands on its own feet, which cannot be said of much that is produced worldwide in the name of children's literature in translation today. There is a growing need to set modern standards for the genre, and Mr Sinha's work has what it takes to do just that.

Much remains to be said, but an adventure story would sag under the weight of a longer introduction. Out with pedantry, then, and in with the tale.

Tathagata Banerjee
Kolkata

The writer is the grandson of Bibhutibhushan Bandopadhyay, and teaches in the Department of English at Bangabasi College in Kolkata.

Note on the Translator

Translation is not just a matter of language. Ideas, images, even daily acts, need translation when they are moved from one culture to another, across space, time and/or media of communication. In its new context, the book, the picture, the notion or the act may acquire new ways of being understood, which were not intended and perhaps cannot even be grasped by the primary artist or thinker. In this sense, one could ask whether it is useful to distinguish the translation from the original; does every use not make a new original? The answer, naturally, is yes and no. *Chander Pahar* has a richness and resonance in the original that is unique; not only in itself, as a work of fiction and as a magnificent adventure story, but also as part of a cherished tradition, as a classic of Bengali 'kumar-sahitya' (young-adult literature), which has been pored over, imagined in dense film-like detail, shared between friends and siblings, and handed down by generations of parents to their children—its lines quotable from memory, each gripping incident inseparable from thousands of private biographies. This was how the translator of this book, my father, described *Chander Pahar* and tried to explain to us what we, his children, were missing and, perhaps, formed the idea of translating it for those who were both deprived of it and deprived of the knowledge of being impoverished.

A translation of *Chander Pahar* cannot be identical to the original; the flavour of the text in translation and the experience of reading it is shaped almost as much by its new linguistic medium and the time and place in which that language is based, as by the original story. Within the fabric of the narrative, some parts will fit easily into the translation while others sag or bulge uncomfortably. Umberto Eco, novelist and theorist of translation and semiotics, described how, when he collaborated with translators who worked his books into their languages, some parts simply had no equivalents in the target language (the language into which the text was being translated) while some translations demanded and wrought new dimensions in the story [*Mouse or Rat? Translation as Discovery* (London: Weidenfeld and Nicolson, 2003)].

If the work of a translation is not to render the original exactly, what is it? Again there is more than one answer, but the best translations seem to evoke a similar or equivalent feeling to the original, whether or not the words are literally transposed. This notion has a special importance in a country like India where so many people translate their thoughts and speech back and forth between two, three or even four languages, and find themselves writing in a language different from or supplementary to their original thoughts. Yet here too, the notions of original and translation, of primary and secondary language can become confused and confusing. For my father's generation, there was a single mother tongue, inherited in infancy, and then there were languages for the outer world, for the business of learning, commerce or travel.

Pradeep Sinha was born in Dibrugarh, Assam, where he learned to speak Bengali and some Assamese. At the age of four, he lost his mother and he and his five brothers were sent away, distributed amongst near relations. My father was put on a train to Calcutta, where he learnt Calcutta Bengali growing up, formal English (at his Jesuit-run school and college) and eventually a Bengali-Bihari variety of Hindi. This was a common pattern for middle-class children raised in urban centres throughout India from the time the colonial system of English education was introduced in the nineteenth century until well after Independence. My father was therefore bilingual, in a way that my brother and I are not. He was born in 1942, the year in which the Indian National Army was raised by Subhash Chandra Bose and the Quit India Movement began under the leadership of Mahatma Gandhi and the Indian National Congress.

By the time he went to school in the 1950s, India had become a Republic and, by 1959, it had an independent constitution. My father grew up between two Indias—one that had internalised completely the ideologies of a colonial state and another that was trying to forge a new political identity among the free young nations of the world. His was a generation that shared the Romantic fascination with the exotic and the mysterious, celebrated in *Chander Pahar*, with the post-Darwinian, late-nineteenth-century engagement with science and society as well as contemporary Indian concerns.

Perhaps it was partly something about being born at a time of political and cultural foment and rebirth, which made my father almost indiscriminately voracious in his curiosity and his eagerness to learn. He read widely in a vast range of subjects, and he read in Bengali as well as English. His translation shows the easy passage of thoughts from one to the other. During a recent reading session of one of his books, Amitav Ghosh answered a question about the naturalness and flow of his own writing in English. He described himself as completely bilingual, and said that the thoughts and conversations he had recorded in the book that he was reading from (set in a small village in Bengal) came to him in both languages and that he could easily move between the two, turning one into the other, and back. This is something I, and many educated Indians my age, cannot do.

My brother and I, for instance, learnt Bengali and English almost simultaneously, then moved from Calcutta to Hyderabad, and, apart from the occasional conversation at home, switched almost entirely to English, and some fragmentary Hindi. Our friends speak English, we read in English, and our stray thoughts as well as our analytical reasoning are in English. When I think about it, I find that my Bengali and my English and my Hindi occupy different parts of my head. We are part of a migrant, mixed urban generation that does not really have a native place or language. My father, like other parents of his generation, was deeply unhappy with our linguistic inability, or rather laziness, and tried to remedy it by speaking with us in Bengali and reading to us what we could not read ourselves. Since we were never ritually inducted into any religion, I imagined that our Sunday readings of Sukumar Ray must have been something like families reading the Bible together; the red-bound, tattered volumes brought down carefully on weekends had an esoteric air of secrets impenetrable unless read aloud by the requisite authority. But the stories and poems read aloud from there, or *Thakumar Jhuri* and other such stories, were in themselves models of clarity and accessibility. Yet, English translations of these works that I have read since have been disappointing because they lacked this quality of readability. And this, precisely, is what is reassuring about Pradeep Sinha's translation of *Chander Pahar*. The language is effortless and simple; its transparent clarity gives free rein to the imaginative force of the story and allows the vivid detail of scenes and episodes to make their own impact.

The Bengali tradition of young-adult literature in fact predates most English stories of the same genre, especially in India, where such books have only recently become widely available in response to a newly perceived market. It is an important in-between age, a time to discover new aspects of the self and identity, when one wants to make journeys into wild places, inward and outward, to find out about the traveller as much as the territory. It is a good time to read *Chander Pahar*, and now is as good a time as any for *Moon Mountain* to be read by those who could not read it in Bengali or even have it read to them when they were young adults, and finally it is a good read for all those who want to experience this classic anew.

ACKNOWLEDGEMENTS

On behalf of Pradeep Sinha, his family would like to thank Mr Taradas Bandopadhyay, the author's son, for his kind permission to translate *Chander Pahar*, and Mr Tathagatha Bandopadhyay, the author's grandson, for contributing a perfectly apposite introduction to the book.

There must be a number of people the translator would have wished to acknowledge for their contribution to making of *Moon Mountain* over the course of several years. Since we may not know all of them, we sincerely apologise for any gaps and omissions that might be perceived in these acknowledgements, and would like to thank those we do know. The translator would have been keen to thank Dr Sujit Mukherjee, who played a vital role in the discussions surrounding the process of translating the book. My family and I cannot find the words to thank Dr Meenakshi Mukherjee for her invaluable help with this project. We would also like to express our gratitude to Mr Samik Ghosh, and all those who helped with and attended the reading of *Moon Mountain* in Hyderabad in the summer of 2006.

Finally, on behalf of the translator and on our own account, we would like to thank the editors, Dr Nandini Rao, Swathi, Parvathy and others at Orient Longman, for their enthusiasm, patience and dedication.

Rajeshwari Mishka Sinha
Cambridge

The writer is the daughter of the translator, Pradeep Sinha, and is currently doing her Ph.D. in English Literature at the University of Cambridge, UK.

A LETTER FROM AFRICA

Shankar was a village boy. He had just passed the F.A. school-leaving examination and had come back to the village to pass time. All morning he visited friends and chatted with them, took a long nap after lunch and then went fishing at the bend of the river in the late afternoon.

When the whole month of Baisakh had passed by thus, his mother said to him one day, 'Listen to me, Shankar, your father hasn't been well at all. I don't see how you can continue your studies. Who is going to pay the expenses? Perhaps you should look for a job.'

What his mother had said made him ponder over his situation. She was right. His father had been quite unwell these past few months. He was having trouble meeting his son's expenses in Calcutta. And yet, what else could Shankar do? Who would give him a job now? He didn't really know anyone who would help.

This was the year 1909. There were still five years to go before the First World War broke out. The job market wasn't so bad in those days.

WESTMARK
WESTMARK'S

There was a man from Shankar's village who worked in a jute mill in either Shyamnagar or Naihati. Shankar's mother met his wife on Shankar's behalf; she hoped the husband could speak to someone and get Shankar a job in his jute mill. The man came to Shankar's house the following day and reassured his mother that he would do his best to get her son a job.

Shankar was no ordinary lad. He always came first in sports at school. In the last district competition, he had won the high jump event and earned himself a medal. There wasn't a football centre-forward like him in that area. Few could equal his swimming talent, and he was an expert in climbing trees, riding and boxing. While studying in Calcutta, he had taken regular boxing lessons at the YMCA. Because of all this he didn't do too well in his examinations. He got a second class.

But there was one subject in which Shankar was uncommonly knowledgeable. It was almost an obsession with him to pore over all sorts of maps and to read large tomes in Geography. He was adept at solving mathematical problems in Geography. He could identify nearly all the stars and constellations visible in the sky—that's Orion, that's Cassiopeia, there's Scorpio, and over there Pegasus—he knew them like the palm of his hand. He knew when they could be seen, he knew the directions from which they rose. He could identify them with just one look at the sky. There were very few young people in our country who could do this.

When he came home from Calcutta this time after his examinations, he had brought with him a pile of books he had bought on these subjects. For hours on end he would sit all by himself and read, lost in his own thoughts. Then came a quick succession of events—his father's illness, the growing poverty of the household, followed soon by his mother's request that he should take up this job in the jute mill. What was he to do? He felt quite helpless. He could not think of disappointing his parents. This meant that he would have to take up this job in the jute mill. That would mean—he knew very well—the end of his dreams. Shankar the famous football centre-forward, the high-jump champion of the district, the reputed swimmer—that Shankar would finally end up as a jute mill clerk! Carrying his tiffin in a book-size tin box and a duster in his pocket, he would rush to the mill as soon as the siren called early in the morning; returning home at noon for a quick meal and back again at two to the mill, to be delivered only by the six o'clock siren.

His fresh young mind couldn't bear to think of such a life. His whole body rebelled at the very thought—would a racehorse end up pulling a hackney-carriage?

The evening drew near. As he sat alone on the river-bank, Shankar's mind was full of these thoughts. In his heart, he wanted to fly, far away to the most distant corners of the earth—amidst the most daring and dangerous happenings—like Livingston and Stanley, like Harry Johnson, Marco Polo and Robinson Crusoe. He had prepared himself for a life of adventure from his childhood. He never stopped to think for a moment that this life of adventure, so possible in the lives of young men of other countries, was practically unthinkable for a boy from Bengal. They were destined to be clerks and school masters or at best, doctors or lawyers. To venture into the unknown and to travel along uncharted routes, was a most unlikely dream.

That night, he opened Westmark's famous book on Geography and began reading it in the dim light of an oil lamp. One part of the book always captivated his mind. This was the strange account by the famous German explorer, Anton Hauptmann, of the ascent of a large mountain in Africa—the Mountain of the Moon. He had read this part several times. Every time he read it, he dreamt that like Hauptmann, he would also go one day to conquer the Mountain of the Moon.

Dreams! He knew now that the real mountains of the moon would always be far away. Would mountains from the moon ever come down to earth ?

That night he had a strange dream. There were thick bamboo forests all around, herds of wild elephants tore down the bamboo. He had someone else with him—they were climbing a huge mountain. The scenery was just as Hauptmann had described in his account of the Mountain of the Moon. The same dense bamboo forests, the huge trees with long overhanging vines, the thick carpet of rotting leaves on the ground, and here and there bare patches of the mountainside, and far away in the distance, washed by moonlight, was the peak of the mountain covered with everlasting snow, now visible through the gaps in the trees, now hidden behind the curtain of the forest. He could almost hear the trumpeting of wild elephants shaking the forest. So real was the trumpeting, that it woke him up. He sat up and saw it was already morning, and the sun flooded the room through the window.

Oh! What a dream! Dreams in the early hours of the morning often come true. That's what people say!

There was an ancient dilapidated temple in their village. Madan Roy, who was one of the Barah Bhuyians of Bengal was said to have built it a long time ago. Madan Roy's family had long gone—the temple was broken and run down; from the cracks in the walls sprouted peepul and banyan trees—but the central dome above the altar had survived. There was no idol—but still people came to the temple to worship every Tuesday and Saturday. Women regularly anointed the altar with vermilion and sandal paste. The reigning deity was known to be benevolent. A wish submitted with a vow was usually granted. After his bath that day, Shankar went to the temple, hung a pebble on a string from one of the overhanging roots of the banyan tree and offered a prayer.

He went back to the temple in the afternoon and sat on the grass in front, for a long time. Although it was a part of the village, the place was surrounded by jungle. There was a broken down old house nearby. Someone had been murdered there when Shankar was a child. The owners had abandoned the house, left the village and were now living somewhere else. People said the place was haunted. Nobody ever came here alone. But Shankar enjoyed the solitude of the temple-courtyard and loved to sit here by himself.

The morning's dream had left a mark on his mind. Sitting in the jungle he remembered it again—the ear-splitting din of wild elephant herds trumpeting and trampling down the huge clumps of bamboo. Far above, glimpsed through the foliage of the dense forest on the mountainside, the snowy peak of the mountain shimmered in the moonlight as if pointing the way to some dreamland. He had dreamt so many dreams but none as vivid as this, and none had made such a deep impression on his mind.

But all this was nonsense! He had to go and work in a jute mill. Wasn't that written in his fate?

But strange and incredible things do actually happen in people's lives. Yet when they are made to happen in novels, readers find them unbelievable and laugh them away. It was just this kind of an incredible event that now occurred quite unexpectedly in Shankar's life.

One morning, just as he was returning home from a walk along the river-bank, Shri Rameshwar Mukherjee's wife, a neighbour, handed him a piece of paper. She said, 'Dear Shankar, at long last we've received news of our son-in-law. His people in Bhadreswar have received a letter. Pintu came from them yesterday and he has brought the address they wrote down for him. Could you read it out to me?'

Shankar said, 'Oh, it must be nearly two years since we have heard from him! How he made everyone worry by running away from home! Didn't he run away once before too?' Then he unfolded the piece of paper. The words on it read, 'Prasad Das Bandopadhyay, Uganda Railway Head Office, Construction Department, Mombasa, East Africa.'

The piece of paper dropped from Shankar's hands. East Africa! Did people run away that far! But he knew that this husband of Nanibaladidi was stubborn, fearless and a vagabond by nature. Shankar had met him once in the village the year he was in Class Ten. The man seemed a large-hearted chap, reasonably well educated but unable to stick to one job for long. He enjoyed a wanderer's life. Once he had left home and gone away to Burma or Cochin or some such place. The last time he disappeared,

Shankar had heard, was after quarelling with his older brother. That same Prasadbabu had now run off all the way to East Africa!

Rameshwar Mukerjee's wife couldn't quite grasp how far her son-in-law had travelled. She simply could not imagine that kind of distance. After she left, Shankar copied the address in his notebook. He wrote to Prasadbabu that very week: 'Did he remember Shankar? He was a boy from his wife's village. He had appeared for his F.A. examination and was now sitting at home. Could Prasadbabu get him a job in his railway company? He was ready to go, no matter how far.'

A month and a half went by and Shankar had almost given up hope of receiving a reply, when a letter arrived in an envelope, addressed to him. It read:

Dear Shankar,

I have received your letter. I remember you very well. I lost to you in arm-wrestling. I haven't forgotten that. You want to come here? Do come. If boys like you don't come out and see the world then who will? A new railway line is being laid here. They need more people. Come as soon as you can. I am taking the responsibility of finding you a job.

Prasad Das Bandopadhyay

Shankar's father was very happy to see the letter. He had also been a daredevil in his youth. He hadn't quite liked the thought of his son going to work in a jute mill and had only agreed with Shankar's mother because of their difficult circumstances.

A month later Shankar received a telegram from Bhadreswar. The son-in-law had arrived. Shankar was to go and see him immediately. He would be returning to Mombasa in another twenty days. He could take Shankar back along with him.

The Camp

Four months later; at the end of March. A branch line was being built from the main track, connecting Mombasa with Kisumu on Lake Victoria and Nyanza. The place was 350 miles west of Mombasa and seventy-two miles south-west of Knudsburg station of the Uganda Railways. Shankar had come there as a clerk and store-keeper in the construction camp. He lived in a small tent. There were a number of other tents around his—no houses had yet been built—arranged in a circle in a large clearing. All around them were stretches of open land, full of tall grass interspersed with a few trees or shrubs. On the outer edge of the tents, where the grassland came to an end, was the famous tree of Africa, the baobab. Shankar had seen it many times in pictures. But now with a real baobab in sight, he could not get enough of it.

In this new country, amidst Uganda's desolate grasslands and forests, Shankar's fresh young mind found a new meaning to his dreams. Every day, soon after work, he would leave the camp and go for long walks. In every direction that he went, there grew grass, as tall as a man, sometimes even taller.

Tirumalappa
Madras
India

The Englishman who was in charge of the construction camp said to him one day, 'Listen Roy, don't go out like you have been doing, over here. You must not step out without a gun. Firstly, you may lose your way in this elephant grass; people have even died of thirst in these parts. Secondly, Uganda is the land of lions. With all of us here and the noise of hammers and steel and of people—the lions may not have approached the camp yet. But they are all around. These Savannahs are not safe at all!'

Work was in full swing one afternoon, when suddenly, a human cry was heard across the grasslands. The men ran to see what had happened. Every bit of the surrounding grassland was combed. Nothing was found.

What were those cries then?

The engineer came, and a roll-call of the coolies was held. One was found missing. On inquiring about him, the engineer was told that the man had gone towards the grassland for something. No one had seen him return.

After searching a great deal, a lion's pug marks were found on the sand just beyond the grass. The engineer went in search of the lion with his gun and a few men. But there was no trace of the animal. Following the pug marks, he found the hapless man behind a large rock. They carried him, mauled and bleeding, back to the tents. The lion had obviously fled upon hearing the cries of the coolies, leaving his prey. The man died before sunset.

The next day, the long grass was cut clean in a wide swathe around the tents. For a few days they talked of little else but the lions. Within a month, however, the story had become stale and no one seemed to remember it. Work resumed as usual.

The days were very hot. But the nights were cool. One evening, the workers had lit a huge fire with lots of dry leaves and branches in front of their tents. They sat around the fire and chatted. Shankar was also there, half-listening to them and also trying to read the *Kenya Morning News* in the fire-light. The newspaper was five days old, but it was the only source of some news from around the world in that faraway place.

Shankar had made friends with a clerk from Madras called Thirumal Appa. Thirumal was a young man. He spoke English quite well and was a spirited fellow. He had run away from home in the hope of adventure. Sitting next to Shankar he talked constantly of his village, of his parents and his little sister. He was especially fond of her. Ever since he left home, he had missed her greatly. He wanted to go home towards the end of September. Would the Engineer sahib deny him a couple of months off?

The night wore on. As the fire died the coolies put in fresh firewood. Most of them went off to sleep. Far in the horizon a broken new moon showed up in the sky. And light and darkness played hide and seek across the vast grassland amidst the long shadows of the trees.

The beauty and the stillness of the night in this strange and far-off land stirred Shankar's soul. Resting his back against a wooden post of the coolie hut, he sat and gazed at the lights and shadows of this vast and uninhabited stretch of the African Savannah—his mind full of thoughts. Beyond that baobab tree the unknown country stretched all the way to Cape Town. On the way would be mountains and numberless forests and the ancient city of Zimbari—the huge and terrifying Kalahari Desert—the land of diamonds, the land of gold!

'Once an adventurer prospecting for gold had suddenly stumbled upon a stone. Examining the stone carefully, he had found traces of gold. And thus, a great gold mine was found at that place.' How many stories like that he had read, back home.

This was that Africa, the dark undiscovered continent, the land of gold, diamond country. How many unknown tribes and landscapes, unseen and unheard birds and animals lay hidden in those boundless tropical forests?

With these thoughts Shankar fell asleep. He woke up with a start. A noise had woken him.The moon had crossed quite a bit of the night-sky. Light from it bathed the whole place, making it look like day. The fire was dead. The coolies were sleeping huddled around the fire. Not a sound anywhere.

Suddenly, Shankar noticed the empty space next to him. Thirumal Appa had been sitting there and chatting with him. Where was he? Maybe he had gone inside the tent to sleep.

Shankar too was thinking of getting up to go inside when there came from the south-west corner of the grassland, the terrifying roar of a lion. The hazy moonlight seemed to tremble with that sound. The coolies woke up startled. The Engineer came out of his tent, gun in hand. This was the first time that Shankar had heard the roar of a lion. In that limitless Savannah, the lion's roar in the moon's fading light evoked strange and indescribable feelings. It was not fear—it was a mysterious complex of emotions. There was an old coolie in the camp who belonged to the Masai tribe. He said a human being had been killed. Not unless he killed a man would a lion roar like that.

Out of the tent Thirumal's companion came, and reported that Thirumal's bed was empty. He was nowhere to be found.

Everyone shuddered. Shankar went into the tent himself and confirmed that Thirumal really wasn't there. The coolies then came out, armed with lights and sticks. Every tent was searched. Thirumal's name was called out from every corner—but there was no sign or sound of him.

The place where Thirumal slept was searched carefully. There were clear signs that something heavy had been dragged over the ground. The conclusions were obvious. A portion of Thirumal's shirt-sleeve was found near the baobab tree. The Engineer went ahead with his gun. Shankar went with him, and the coolies followed. In the dead of the night a wide area around the tents was thoroughly searched, but no trace of Thirumal's body could be found. The lion's roar was heard again, but from a distance. It sounded like the blood-curdling shriek of the demon-queen of this bleak and desolate countryside.

The Masai coolie said 'The lion is taking the body away. But he will trouble us yet. He won't leave us without making a few more attacks on our men. So please be very careful. Once a lion starts killing humans, he becomes very sly and cunning.'

It was almost three in the morning when everyone returned to camp. Moonlight had flooded the entire countryside. Birds were usually not seen during the day in this part of Africa—but there was a species of nocturnal bird whose cries could be heard at night—it had an unearthly sweetness. Just then one of those birds sang from a distant tree. Shankar's mind was filled with a strong foreboding. He didn't go back to sleep. Everyone else went into their tents—they were all tired. A huge fire was again lit with logs and branches. Shankar, of course, didn't have the courage to sit outside—that would have been foolhardy. But he lay down in his tent and gazed out of the window into the mysterious grassland bathed in moonlight. Thirumal was dead. Was it for this that his destiny dragged him so far into the depths of Africa?

Africa is a beautiful, terrifying country. The Savannah may look like the meadows of Bengal filled with acacia trees—but it was unknown and deadly dangerous. All around there lurked unseen dangers that spelled swift and terrible death.

Africa had claimed her first victim—the young Indian, Thirumal. She wanted more.

From the next day the marauding lions made life in the camp intolerable. A man-eating lion is a most dangerous animal—as cunning as he is daring. It wasn't even possible to go out alone during the day any more. Before darkness fell, fires were lit in several places around the camp, everyday. The coolies would huddle close to the fires and cook, talk and eat there. The Engineer would make three or four rounds of the camp every night, gun in hand, and fire a few blanks. In spite of all these precautions, the lion grabbed another coolie early in the evening just two days after it had killed Thirumal.

The next day, a Somali labourer had gone to break stones in a boulder-heap just three hundred yards from the camp. He didn't come back in the evening.

One night Shankar was returning from the Engineer's tent at about ten. Most of the people in the camp had retired early. Only a few were still outside huddled around the dying fires. From a distance came the howling of jackals. Whenever he heard jackals howling Shankar felt as if he was back in his village in Bengal. He would close his eyes and try to remember his village. He would think of the hog-plum tree that stood in the corner of his house. He stopped walking and closed his eyes.

What a lovely feeling it was. Where was he? Sleeping on his cot next to the window in his village home. If he opened his eyes the branches of the hog-plum tree would surely come into view. Should he open his eyes and see? Slowly he opened them.

The grassland was dark. In the misty darkness the baobab tree in the distance looked like a standing giant. Suddenly he thought he saw something move on the round thatch roof of one of the huts. Immediately, he turned numb with fear and awe.

A huge lion was trying to part the thatch with its paws. From time to time, it would push its nose into the hole it had made and smell something.

The hut was no more than twenty yards from where he was standing.

Shankar knew he was in grave danger. The lion was busy trying to make an opening in the thatch. It would enter the hut through the hole and grab another victim. There was not a soul outside the tents. Terrified by lions, everyone had retired early. He was alone, unarmed. But the lion hadn't seen Shankar yet.

With his eyes glued to the animal, Shankar began to walk silently backwards towards the Engineer's tent. One minute...two minutes...Shankar never knew he had such control over his nerves. He didn't allow any sound of his overpowering fear to escape his lips. Nor did he try to suddenly turn and run away.

Lifting the curtains of the Engineer's tent, he found him still at his table, working. Before the Sahib could look surprised at his behavior and ask, Shankar said, 'Sahib, lion.'

The Engineer sprang up and said 'What? Where?'

In the gun-rack was a .375 Mannlicher rifle. The Sahib grabbed that and gave Shankar another gun. The two of them lifted the tent curtains and emerged cautiously. The round thatch of the coolie hut was a short distance away. But where was the lion? Shankar said 'I saw it just now, Sir. It was trying to break through the thatch with its paws.'

The Sahib said 'It has run away. Wake everyone up.'

Soon the entire camp was in an uproar. Troop of coolies came out shouting, armed with sticks, spears, pickaxes and clubs. They searched everywhere. The hole in the thatch was discovered, so were the lion's pug marks. But the lion had vanished. The fires were lit again with more leaves, branches and firewood. No one slept that night, but no one stayed out either. Towards the morning when Shankar had just fallen asleep in his tent, he was woken up by a big commotion. The Masai coolies were screaming—'Simba, Simba.' A gun was fired twice. He came out of his tent and on inquiry learnt that the lion had raided the stables a little while ago and wounded a pack-mule. It had happened just when people were dozing off towards the morning.

The next day, at about dusk, the lion carried away a young coolie within a hundred yards of the camp. Four days later another coolie was taken from under the baobab.

The coolies no longer wanted to work. Those with pickaxes sometimes had to work in very small groups. They now refused to work far away from the camp even during the day. Even the camp was not safe at night. Each one feared that his turn would be next. No work was done. Only the Masai remained calm. They feared not even Yama. They were the only coolies who would agree to work with pickaxes two miles away from the camp. The Engineer would go four or five times a day, gun in hand, to see them.

A number of new arrangements were made, none worked. The lion menace continued unabated. Some said 'There is not just one lion but many. How many can one kill?' And the Sahib said 'There are never a lot of man-eaters. All this is just one lion's doing.'

One day the engineer asked Shankar to take a gun and go and have a look at the group working with pickaxes.

Shankar said 'Sahib, please let me have your Mannlicher.'

He agreed. Shankar got on a mule with the gun and started off. About a mile from the camp was a small lake. It was about three o'clock in the afternoon when Shankar was within sight of the lake. Not a soul was around; the scorching sun raised currents of hot air in the open Savannah.

Suddenly the mule stopped. It just wouldn't go any further. Shankar felt the mule was afraid to go towards the lake. At that moment, something stirred in the nearby bush. He turned and looked but could not see anything. He got off the mule. Still the animal wouldn't move.

Suddenly Shankar's whole body trembled as if he had been struck by a live wire. Was the lion lying in wait behind the bush? He knew that lions are known to stalk their prey in total silence for long distances, hiding behind bushes and shrubs. What if the lion, seeing an opportunity in this secluded spot, sprang on him? Shankar felt it would not be wise to go any further with the mule. He decided to turn back. He had just turned the mule towards the camp when he saw something stir in the bush once again. In a flash—there was a mighty roar and a massive sand-coloured body fell on the mule with a heavy thud. Shankar was hardly a couple of yards ahead. He immediately turned round and fired twice. He wasn't sure if the bullets had found their mark, but the mule had crumpled to the ground and the lion had vanished. Shankar examined the mule's wounds—one shoulder was ripped through and the ground beneath was soaked with blood. The mule was writhing in pain. Shankar put an end to its agony with a bullet. He returned to the camp.

The Sahib said the lion must have been badly wounded. But did the bullets hit the lion? Shankar said he wasn't sure of that. He was only certain that he had fired. A number of people searched all around for the next two or three days, but neither a wounded nor a dead lion was found.

In early June the rains started. Partly on account of the man-eating lions and partly because of its proximity to a lake which had become unhealthy in the rainy season, the camp moved away.

Shankar did not have to stay in the construction camp any longer. He took his stuff and moved to a small railway station about thirty miles from Kisumu, where he was given the job of station-master.

The Station

When Shankar arrived at the small railway station, happy with his new job, it was about three in the afternoon. The station was very small. The platform was made of earth. The station-office and platform were surrounded by a barbed-wire fence. His living quarters were behind the station office—a small pigeon-hole of a room. The train that brought him there continued on its way to Kisumu. Shankar felt as if he was stranded in the middle of a limitless ocean. Even in his imagination he couldn't think of a lonelier place.

He was the only official in this railway station. There wasn't even a coolie. He was the coolie, the pointsman, he was everybody!

This was because small stations were not profitable at all. They existed only as experimental stops. The railway company was not willing to spend much money on them. One train in the morning and the one that had dropped Shankar off, in the afternoon—that was all.

Shankar, therefore, had a lot of time to spare. All he needed to do was to understand and take charge of his duties. His predecessor was a Gujarati. He knew English

fairly well. This Gujarati gentleman was very happy to have him around. It seemed he hadn't had anyone to talk to for a long time. They paced the platform from one end to the other.

Shankar asked, 'Why the barbed-wire fence?'

The Gujarati gentleman said 'That's nothing. It's just that it's a lonely place.'

Shankar felt the man was not telling him everything. But he didn't persist. At night the gentleman made chapatis, and invited Shankar to dinner. He suddenly said 'How terrible, I've forgotten.'

'What happened?'

'There is no drinking water. I completely forgot to take some down from the train.'

'Why? Is there no place to get water from around here?'

'There is a well, but its water is bitter and alkaline. That water is fit only for washing. Drinking water comes by the train.'

What a place! No drinking water, no human beings! Shankar wondered why they had built a station there.

The following morning, the previous station master left. Now Shankar was all alone. He did his work, cooked for himself and stood at the platform when it was time for the trains. In the afternoons he read or had a snooze, lying on the big table. Later, when the platform came into the shade, he took a walk there.

All around the station was the limitless grassland—forests of tall grass, here and there a few yuca and acacia trees—and in the distance were rows of mountains, spread across the entire horizon. A marvellous sight.

The Gujarati gentleman had warned him that he should never go out alone into these grasslands.

Shankar had asked 'But why?' He did not get a satisfactory reply to his question from the Gujarati gentleman, but received an answer the same night, from another quarter.

After an early dinner, Shankar had lit the lamp in the station-office and was writing his diary. He had planned to sleep there. The room, with glass panes, was closed but not bolted. A sound made him look up at the door—he saw a huge lion looking in with its muzzle against the glass. Shankar froze in his chair. A gentle push would open the door, and he was completely unarmed! There was only a wooden ruler on the table.

The lion stood there silently, looking at Shankar and at the kerosene lamp on the table, with a curious expression. He wasn't there for long—perhaps a couple of minutes—but Shankar felt as if they had been staring at each other for ages. Then the lion went away as if disinterested in what he saw.

Shankar suddenly recovered his wits and quickly bolted the door.

Now, he said to himself, he understood the significance of the barbed-wire fence around the station. But Shankar was wrong—he had got only a partial answer to his question. He had to wait for a couple of days to get the rest of the answer.

It came from a totally different quarter.

The next day, he told the guard of the morning train about his adventures of the previous night. The guard was a good man. He listened to Shankar's tale and then said, 'In these parts, it's the same story everywhere. There is another small station like yours about twelve miles from here, there too it's the same situation. In fact it so happened . . .'

He was about to say something, but stopped himself and quickly got into the train. As the train moved away, he called out, 'Be very careful, all the time.'

Shankar felt worried. What were they trying to hide? Were there other dangers besides the lion? Anyway, from that day, Shankar started lighting a fire in the station-office before dark and read or wrote his dairy till late at night.

The nights were dark in the boundless Savannah. The night winds, caught between the leaves of the yuca tree on the platform, made a strange noise; the jackals howled periodically, and sometimes in the middle of the night one could hear the roar of the lion.

But this was the life he had wanted. It was in his blood. This desolate grassland, its mysterious nights, its sky full of unknown stars and lurking dangers—this was life!

One day Shankar had seen off the afternoon train and was about to enter the kitchen in his quarters, when suddenly he saw something against the wooden post and took a mighty leap backwards. A huge yellow and brown cobra stood, hood expanded, hardly a foot from the post. 'If I had seen it two seconds later, then? Anyway, now what do I do about the snake?' he thought. But the next moment the snake climbed up the post and disappeared into the thatch roof. What a thing to happen! Shankar had to go into the kitchen and cook. This was not a lion that could be kept out by a fire and a closed door. Shankar hesitated for a while but finally decided to go into the kitchen. He hurriedly cooked his meal and finished his dinner before it grew dark. Then he came out of his quarters and went into the station-office. But what was so safe about the station-office? Snakes could come in through any crack or hole anytime. There was no stopping them.

The next day, a new coolie came on the morning train to unload his provisions from the guard's carriage. Twice a week, the Railway Company sent rice and potatoes from Mombasa to its employees in out-of-the-way places. The price was deducted from their monthly salaries.

The new coolie was an Indian from Gujarat. After unloading the provision sacks, he looked very strangely at Shankar. And just in case Shankar asked him something, he hurried back into the train.

Shankar hadn't missed the strange look in the man's eyes. No one was willing to tell him what mysteries were connected with this place. It was as if talking about it was against the rules. What was all this about?

A couple of days later, he had green-signalled the train and was returning to his quarters, when he almost stepped on a yellow and brown cobra. It could have been the earlier cobra, but there was no telling.

That day Shankar carefully examined the ground around the station, the floors of the station-office and of his quarters. He found large holes everywhere on the ground. The courtyard of the quarters, the walls of the kitchen and the unpaved platform were riddled with holes and cracks, and strewn with the droppings of rats. But he didn't understand the significance of this yet.

One night he was sleeping in the station-office. He suddenly woke up. The room was dark. It was as if a sixth sense had woken him up for a moment to warn him that he was in grave danger. In the pitch darkness, Shankar felt his whole body trembling. Why couldn't he find the torch? There was a faint noise in the room. Suddenly his groping hand found the torch, and he flashed it on.

In the same instant he froze, numb with fear and awe.

Midway between the wall and his bed, there stood, with its hood held high but temporarily dazed by the light of the torch, Africa's meanest and most fearsome snake—the black mamba. The hood rose almost a metre from the floor. This was not unusual because a black mamba usually strikes on the shoulders. To escape from a black mamba is like being born again, Shankar had heard.

From his boyhood, Shankar had one great quality. He never lost his head when in danger. He could exercise complete control over his nerves in the gravest of situations.

Shankar knew that if his hands shook even a little—and the light moved away from the eyes of the snake—it would come out of its temporary daze and immediately strike.

He realised that his life depended on his ability to keep the light firmly and steadily trained on the snake's eyes. As long as he could hold the torch in that position, he was safe. But what if his hands shook?

Shankar held on to the torch. The snake's eyes burned like two round points of light. What terrible power and anger seemed to come out of that thick black body, standing upright like a rigid whip.

Shankar had forgotten the furniture in the room, the continent of Africa, his railway job, the rail track from

Mombasa to Kisumu, his country, his parents—the world vanished and was transformed into those two small luminous spheres. There was nothing beyond! Total darkness. As empty as death, and as dark as the universe after a cataclysm.

The only truth was the ferociously-hooded, strike-ready mamba, which could inject 1500 milligrams of lethal venom with a single bite and which was waiting there, ready for him.

Shankar's hand ached, his fingers were becoming numb. He had lost all sensation from elbow to shoulder. How long had he to keep holding the torch? Those two specks of light were probably not the eyes of a snake—but fireflies or distant stars, or even . . .

Weren't the torch-batteries losing their power? Wasn't the white light becoming dim and yellow? But the fireflies or stars were shining on just as before. Was it night or day? Was he waiting for the morning or the evening?

Shankar took hold of himself. He felt as if those two burning eyes had hypnotised him. He must be alert. He knew that in this god-forsaken place there was no one to hear him even if he screamed. His life depended on how strong his nerves were. But he felt he couldn't keep this up much longer. His hands were becoming increasingly numb with pain. Let the snake bite; better to give his aching hands some rest and relief.

Just then the clock began to strike three in the morning. Shankar was probably meant to live only till three, because as soon as the clock struck, his hand shook and moved a little. The two specks of light disappeared; but where was the snake? Why didn't it strike?

It took Shankar a moment to understand that the snake too had become temporarily dazed like him. This was his chance. Lightning fast he jumped from the table, unlocked the door in the dark, went out and locked the door from the outside.

The morning train came. Shankar had spent the night on the platform. He recounted the entire event to the guard. The guard said, 'Come, let's have a look at the station-office.' But no trace of the snake could be found in the room. The guard was a nice man, he said—'Listen, you had a narrow escape last night. I hadn't told you till now, thinking I might frighten you, that the gentleman who was the station-master before you ran away because of the snakes. Before that, two previous station-masters had died of snake-bite in the station-quarters. In Africa, people don't venture anywhere near places where there are black mambas. I am talking to you as a friend, please don't tell the bosses that you have heard all this from me. Apply for a transfer.'

Shankar said, 'It will take a long time to get a reply to my application. In the meantime, please do me a favour. I am completely unarmed here, get me a gun or a revolver on your next trip, and some carbolic acid. Please let me have the carbolic acid positively on your way back.'

He requisitioned one of the coolies from the train, and the two of them spent the whole day sealing all the holes on the ground. Careful examination seemed to indicate that the mamba had come out of a hole in the corner of the western wall of the station-office. Most of the holes were rat-holes. The snake had probably entered them during the day to look for a rat. Shankar filled up the holes with care. He got a bottle of carbolic acid from the down-train guard, and sprinkled the acid all over the room as well as around the room. The coolie left him a stout wooden staff. Within the next three days, he got a gun from the railway company.

FINDING ALVAREZ

Water was a big problem at the station. The water that the train provided was just about enough for cooking and drinking. There wasn't any left for a bath. The local well had also dried up. One day Shankar heard that there was a lake about three miles from the station. The water was good and there were fish in the lake.

Lured by the prospects of a bath and a chance to fish, Shankar set off one morning in search of the lake after signalling off the train. He took with him a Somali coolie, to show him the way. He had arranged for the fishing gear to be brought from Mombasa. The lake was of a middling size. All around were forests of tall grass and yuca trees. Close by was a hillock. After a bath in its waters he fished for a couple of hours and caught a number of small fish. Although he had not fished for a long time, he felt he couldn't sit there much longer. He had to be back at the station by four to signal the afternoon train.

After that, he often went fishing and bathing in the lake. Sometimes he had someone with him—but mostly he went alone.

Mithila M.

The African summer was extremely fierce. It was now impossible to go out after nine in the morning. After eleven, Shankar felt as if the surroundings had caught fire. Yet he heard from people in the trains that this was nothing compared to the heat in Central and Southern Africa.

It was around this time that an event took place which completely changed the pace and direction of Shankar's life. One morning he had gone fishing. When he was on his way back, it was about three in the afternoon. The station was still about a mile away when Shankar heard someone calling out in a faint voice from somewhere across the scorching grassland. Then, he saw a man sitting in the sparse shade of a yuca tree.

Shankar quickened his pace and approached him. The man was European. He wore a dirty coat and a pair of ragged and patched up trousers. Although he looked thin and emaciated from hunger, heat and illness, it was quite apparent that he had once been strong and robust. He leaned against the trunk of the tree, looking totally exhausted. His dirty sola hat had slipped off his head and was lying on the ground. Next to him was a large bundle of khaki cloth.

Shankar spoke in English 'Where are you coming from?'

The man didn't answer but, putting his hand to his mouth, said 'Water, water please.'

Shankar said, 'There is no water here. Can you come up to the station leaning on me?'

With great difficulty, partly leaning on Shankar, and towards the end, almost on Shankar's shoulders, the man reached the platform. Bringing him across delayed Shankar and he found that the afternoon train had come and gone in his absence. He made a bed for the man in the station-office and made him lie down. After taking a drink of water and some food, he recovered a bit but Shankar saw that the man had high fever. Many days of physical strain and hunger had completely broken him. He was not going to be all right in three or four days.

After a while the man began to talk. His name was Diego Alvarez—he was Portuguese, though the African sun had tanned his skin to a coppery brown.

That night Shankar kept him in the station. But he was worried. There were no medicines, no doctors around. The morning train did not go towards Mombasa, although the guard in the afternoon train could pick him up the next day. But the whole night had to pass before that.

Shankar spent the entire night nursing the sick man. Such a long way from home, and he had no one. If Shankar didn't look after him, who would?

Ever since he was a child, Shankar couldn't bear to see people suffer. Diego's own people could not have looked after him any better than the way Shankar nursed him the whole night.

That night the moon had climbed up from behind the low hills on the north-east horizon and the grassland shimmered in the eerie moonlight. Suddenly from across the Savannah came the powerful roar of lions. Diego, who had been half-asleep, sat up with a start. Shankar said, 'Don't worry lie down. The lions are out in the grassland. The door is bolted.' Then Shankar softly opened the door, came out and stood on the platform. He was fascinated by the beauty of the night. The moon was in a distant corner of the sky, and the moonlight threw the long shadows of the yuca trees from the east to the west. The grassland looked still and mysterious. The roar of the lions came from behind the station-quarters, about five hundred yards away. But Shankar had become used to the sound—he was not frightened by it anymore. He was so enchanted by the night's beauty that he almost forgot about the lions.

He went back to the station-office. The clock struck two. When he entered the room he found Diego was still sitting up on his bed. He said, 'Please give me some water to drink.'

The traveller could speak English quite well. Shankar drew some water out of the tin and gave it to him.

The fever seemed to have subsided. The man said, 'What were you saying? You thought I was afraid?

Diego Alvarez afraid? Young man you don't know Diego Alvarez.' On the corner of his lips was a strange smile—it was a mixture of disappointment, sorrow and sarcasm. He fell back on his pillow exhausted. That smile told Shankar that this was no ordinary man. Then he noticed his hands. Short, stubby fingers, and his arms were criss-crossed with varicose veins. The chin behind the copper-coloured beard spoke of a strong personality. As the fever came down, the real person slowly emerged.

The man said, 'Come near me. You have done me a great favour. My own son could not have done more. But let me tell you something—I am not going to live. I feel my days are over. Are you an Indian? How much do you earn here? If you have come this far from your country for this small salary, then you surely have the courage and the ability to bear hardship. Listen to me carefully, but promise me that whatever I tell you today, you will not disclose to anyone before I die.'

Shankar promised. Then, as that eventful night slowly wore on, Shankar found himself listening to a most fantastic and incredible story—such as one reads only in books of fiction.

DIEGO'S STORY:

'Young man, how old are you? Twenty-two? When you were a baby in your mother's arms—twenty-two years ago—around 1888–89, I was prospecting for gold in the jungles among the mountains to the north of Cape Colony. I too was young then; no danger in the world was dangerous enough for me to take heed of.

I had bought all my provisions in Bulwaye and set off alone. I took with me only two donkeys to carry my things. I crossed the Zambesi and moved on through completely unknown country and tracks. On the way were small hills, grassland and some scattered Kaffir villages. Gradually I left all human habitation behind and came to a place where no European had set foot before.

Wherever I came across a river or stream—or even a hill—I searched for veins of gold. So many people had made discoveries and become rich in South Africa. I had heard countless such stories in my childhood. It was the lure of these tales that had drawn me to Africa. But in vain did I spend two years roaming around. What terrible hardships I suffered. Once I even stumbled on a find, but then lost it again.

I remember one morning I had killed an antelope. I pitched tent, cooked the meat and lay down because, in that part of Africa, it is impossible to be out in the afternoon sun. The temperature ranges from 115 to 130 degrees farenheit in summer. After a bit of rest, I thought I would clean the gun. Then, I discovered that the gun-sight was missing from the barrel. You cannot aim a gun without a sight-hole. I searched all around but couldn't find the gun-sight. Nearby was a little mound. Along the sides of the mound, I found some small, white, hard stones. I selected one of those small stones and, after some rubbing and scraping, fitted that on to the barrel as a gun-sight. Then, late in the afternoon, I set off again towards the north. In course of time I completely forgot where I had pitched tent, near that mound with stones.

In about a fortnight I met an Englishman. Like me, he was searching for gold. With him he had two Matabele coolies. We were very happy to have met each other. His name was Jim Carter. He was a vagabond like me, only much older. One day he took my gun to have a look. Suddenly he peered at it and looked very surprised— "Why is your eye-piece like this?" he asked. When he heard my story he was very excited. He said, "You don't recognise this?—it's pure silver ore. Wherever this substance is found, there are silver deposits. From every tonne of this quality of ore you can recover at least nine thousand ounces of pure silver! Let's go there at once. We could become millionaires!"

Let me cut this short. After that I took Carter along and went back the same way that I came. For four months we tried very hard. A number of times we almost died, losing our way in the boundless, desert-like Veldt. Yet, I just could not find the place. When I had struck camp there for the last time, I did not take care to notice my surroundings. In any case there are few landmarks, in the African Veldt, by which one can relocate a place. Every place looks the same. Having failed to find the silver mines after a number of attempts, we lost hope and travelled towards the River Gwai. Jim Carter did not leave me. He was with me till his death. I still feel depressed when I think of his terrible death.

The one thing that troubled us most on that journey was the scarcity of water. So we decided we would travel along the river. We lived mainly by hunting animals in the forests. Sometimes, if we came across a Kaffir village, we could get sweet potatoes and chicken.

Once, we had crossed the River Orange and had taken shelter in a Kaffir village about fifty miles from the river. That night the daughter of the village chief became violently ill. We went to see her. A little girl about five or six years old, with no clothes on, was writhing on the floor. She complained of a severe stomach ache. Every one was weeping and moving around aimlessly. They said some evil spirit must have come upon the child and would not leave without killing her. All that her parents could tell us was that she had gone towards the forest and had come back with the evil spirit in her.

Seeing her condition, I guessed she must have had too much of some fruit or berry. We asked her if she had eaten any fruits in the forest. She said "Yes." "Raw fruits?" She said "No, not the fruit, but the seeds."

We were carrying a box of medicines with us. One dose of homeopathic medicine drove out the evil spirit. We stayed on in the village for another fifteen days as the honoured guests of the chief. We would often go out and shoot an Eland antelope, and invite the villagers for a meal.

When we were leaving, the Kaffir chief said, "You like white stones, I know. They are nice to play with. You want some? Wait, let me show you."

Soon he brought us a white stone the size of a marble. Jim and I were awestruck—that was a diamond! It was an uncut and unpolished diamond—the kind that you get from the surface of a mine.

The Kaffir chief said "Please take this. Can you see those mountains in the distance, a little hazy from here? Walking from here you can reach them in one moon. I have heard that the mountain is full of these white stones. We have never been there. It is not a good place. It is the den of the evil spirit—*Bunip*. Many moons ago, three brave men from our village defied everyone and went to that mountain—and never returned. Another time a white man like you had come; that also was many, many moons ago. It was in my grandfather's time. He too never returned."

Leaving the Kaffir village, we consulted the map and found that the hazy distant shapes were the Richtersveld range—South Africa's wildest, most unknown, massive and terribly dangerous area. Apart from a few fearless explorers and geographers, no civilised man had set foot in those parts. Jungles covered the mountains, and that vast terrain was completely unexplored. There were no maps and no routes.

The blood in our veins raced. We decided at that very moment that those mountains and jungles were hiding their fabulous treasures from the eyes of other men, waiting for us alone. We must go there.

We trekked for about seventeen days from the Kaffir village and reached the dense forests at the foot-hills of the mountain range.

I had mentioned to you earlier that these mountains were located in one of the most remote parts of Southern Africa. We couldn't find a single Kaffir village near those forests. Not even a wood-cutter's axe had seen the inside of that jungle.

We had reached the jungle a little before dusk. On Jim Carter's advice we pitched our tent there to rest for the night. Jim collected some firewood and built a fire. I set about cooking dinner. That morning we had shot a couple of birds. I planned to clean and roast them. I was busy dressing the birds when Jim said "Leave the birds, why don't you make two cups of coffee." The fire was lit already. I put the water to boil and, as I went back to cleaning the birds, we heard the roar of lions from somewhere quite close. Jim went out with his gun. I warned him "It's getting dark, don't go far." Soon, I heard the gun being fired twice from a little distance away. Then complete silence. When ten minutes had passed and Jim did not return, I took my own rifle and set out in the direction of the gunshots. Before I could go far, I saw Jim coming back dragging something heavy. On seeing me, he said, "Beautiful skin. If I left it in the jungle, the hyenas would have finished it. Let's drag it to the tent." The two of us dragged the huge carcass of a lion to the fire near our tent. As evening grew into night we finished our dinner and went to sleep.

Late at night the roar of lions woke us up. They seemed quite close to the camp. In the darkness we couldn't make out how close. I held my rifle and sat on my bed. Jim just said, "It's the mate of the lion I killed in the evening."

Having said this, he calmly fell asleep. I went out of the tent and saw that the fire had gone out. There were some logs nearby. I lit the fire again and went back to sleep.

The next morning we entered the forest. After a while, we met some Kaffirs. They had come to hunt deer. We tried to persuade them to come with us and be our coolies and guides, by offering them tobacco.

They said, "You are saying this because you are ignorant. No humans come to these forests. If you value your lives, go back. Beyond that low hill there is some flat land surrounded by dense forests, and beyond that are high mountains. That flat land is very dangerous. The Bunip lives there. If the Bunip catches you, you are finished—you will not return. No one goes there. Do you think we'll go there to die, for some tobacco? If you know what's good for you, you won't go either."

We asked "What's a Bunip?"

They didn't know. But they said very clearly that even if they didn't know what a Bunip was, they knew only too well what damage it could do.

We had never known fear—Jim Carter was particularly brave. He became even more determined. He must unravel the mystery of this Bunip—it didn't matter whether we found diamonds or not. If only I had understood then that, unknown to him, death was drawing him near.'

At this point in the narrative, the old man had become breathless. Shankar's curiosity had been thoroughly aroused by then. He had never heard anything like this before! Looking at the dying Diego Alvarez's ragged clothes, his venous hands and the two bright steel-blue eyes under a pair of bushy white eyebrows, Shankar was filled with affection and admiration for the man.

Here was a real man!

Alvarez said 'Another glass of water, please.' He drank the water and continued his story.

'So listen to what happened after that. We entered the dense forest. Huge trees, gigantic ferns, so many orchids and lianas of different colours. The forest, in places, was so dense with trees and shrubs that it was almost impassable. The overhang of branches and leaves was entangled with thorny shrubs, so that sunlight could hardly penetrate those jungles. The sky was invisible. Baboons were a great menace all over the forest. They lived in hordes—babies, young ones, grown ups and the elderly, all sitting on branches. Most of the time they seemed undaunted at the approach of humans—they would bare their teeth to frighten us. A few of the old leader baboons were really fierce—if we didn't have guns they would surely have attacked us. Jim Carter said, "At least we'll never be short of food in this jungle."

We spent seven or eight days in that dense forest. Jim Carter was right—everyday a baboon had to die to provide us with food. A number of small and big streams flowed down from the mountain tops through various parts of the forest. So we were never short of drinking water. But water did pose a problem once. One afternoon we had made a fire next to a stream and were about to roast the thigh of a baboon, when Jim felt very thirsty and drank some water from the stream. Soon after he felt sick and started retching. He also had excruciating pain in the stomach. I had some medical knowledge. Suspecting that something was wrong with the water, I tested it and found it had arsenic dissolved in it. There must have been layers of arsenic on the summit of the mountain and the stream was washing it down. I gave him an antidote from my box of homeopathic medicines. Jim recovered by evening.

In that dense jungle we didn't come across any wild animals except baboons and a few poisonous snakes. Of course, I am not counting the multi-coloured birds and butterflies we encountered, which are not generally categorised as wild animals.

We first came across a branch of the Richtersveld mountain range. Although it was parallel to the main and original range, it was less in height. Going across that, we descended into a large forested valley and camped there. A stream flowed down the middle of the valley. Both Jim and I were delighted to see the small river. It is along the banks of such rivers that one discovers mineral ores.

We examined the sand at several points along the river but could not find anything. There wasn't even a trace of gold in the sands. After some time we gave up hope. By then at least three weeks had gone by. One evening, while having coffee, Jim said "Look, I have a feeling we will find gold here. Let's stay here for a few more days." Another twenty days passed. Baboon meat had become unbearable and totally unpalatable. Even Jim lost hope.

I said, "Jim, there is no point trying anymore. Let's go back. We were taken for a ride by the Kaffir villagers. There is nothing here."

Jim said, "This mountain range has a number of branches. I will not leave until I have seen all of them."

One day, while panning the sand sitting on the bank of an inlet of the river, both Jim and I simultaneously noticed a small yellow stone half-buried under a pile of pebbles. We quickly dug it out. Our faces glowed with happiness and wonder. Jim said, "Diego, our labours have at last been rewarded. Do you recognise this?"

Of course I had recognised it. I said "Yes, but this has been carried down the river by the current. There is no mine here."

The stone was of one variety of the famous yellow diamond of South Africa. Actually there wasn't much cause for rejoicing. All that it proved was that somewhere in those unknown, impassable mountains, there was a diamond mine. A broken piece of the strata had flowed down with the river current. It would take superhuman efforts to find the original mine.

We did not lack that effort, patience or courage. But the Bunip, guardian of the priceless diamond mines of that mysterious mountain and forest, obstructed us most unexpectedly.

One day towards the evening we were resting in a clearing in the forest. Close to where we sat, there was a palm tree. Around the tree were very thick bushes. Suddenly we noticed the palm tree was shaking violently, the dry leaves on the topmost branches rustling loudly. It was exactly as if it was struck by a storm. The whole tree was swaying.

We were very surprised. There was no breeze. Why was the palm tree swaying? It was almost as if someone was holding the trunk and shaking it. Jim immediately went to investigate and entered the dense thicket around the palm tree.

Soon after he went in, I heard a cry of pain and ran towards the sound with my gun. Upon entering the bushes I found Jim lying inside, mortally wounded. Some extremely powerful animal had ripped and lacerated the flesh from his face to his chest with razor sharp claws—it was like tearing open and exposing the stuffing inside an old pillow.

Jim only said, "Devil incarnate! Satan himself!"—then indicated with his hands—run away, run away.

Jim died soon after. I found some large thorns stuck on the truck of the palm tree. It seemed that some immensely strong animal had been rubbing itself against the trunk of the tree and that was why the tree was swaying. I could find no trace of the animal. I dragged Jim's body out into the open and then went to the other side of the bush, rifle in hand. There I found the footprints of some unknown animal—it had only three toes. I followed the footprints for some distance, till they disappeared into a cave. At the entrance of the cave, on the dry sand, I found clear prints of this three-toed beast.

It had become dark by then. I was all alone in that desolate forest, in an unknown valley surrounded by mountains, trying to track an even more unknown and immensely powerful animal. In the fading light of dusk I saw, to my right, a steep perpendicular cliff of basalt–almost four thousand feet high and capped with dense forests. At its summit, above the forest of bamboo, there was a faint reddish glow of sunlight—or perhaps my eyes were deceiving me and it was just the reflected glow of the infinite sky.

I did not think it prudent to either enter the cave or wait at the entrance, at that time of the day. I returned to the camp with Jim's body. I made a fire, and sat there with him the whole night, ready with my rifle.

The next day I buried Jim, and set out again to look for that animal. However much I searched, I just could not find that cave again. There were so many similar caves at various places among those mountains. Who knows which cave I had seen in the evening darkness.

Without a companion it was not possible to remain in the Richtersveld mountains. After a fifteen-day walk I reached the Kaffir village where we had made a stop. They recognised me and gave me a warm welcome. I told them the story of Jim's death.

When they heard my story their faces wore looks of intense fear. Their small eyes became big with apprehension. They said, "What a calamity! Bunip! It's for fear of the Bunip that no one goes there."

From the Kaffir village, I walked for another five days to reach the Orange River where I caught a Dutch launch. The launch brought me back to civilisation.

I could not journey towards the Richtersveld mountains again, though I tried very hard. The war came in between. I enlisted. I was wounded, and had to stay in a hospital in Pretoria for many months. When I recovered, I got a job in an orange plantation and was there all these years.

After four or five years of peaceful life I became bored, so I set out again. I have become old, young man, I think my journeys are coming to an end.

Keep this map with you. It contains a rough sketch of the Richtersveld mountains and that of the river where we found the diamond. If you have the courage, go there. You'll become a rich man. After the Boer War, a few big and some small diamond mines have been discovered around the River Wait, but no one knows about the place we found. You should go there.'

Diego Alvarez completed his story and leaning back on his pillow lay down again, exhausted.

The Lost Mine

Shankar's nursing and care helped Diego Alvarez recover from his illness. For the next fortnight or so Shankar persuaded Diego to stay with him. But having been a wanderer all his life, he could hardly settle down to a domestic life. He became impatient to go out again. Shankar had already made up his mind about his next course of action. He said to Alvarez, 'Do you remember all that you said to me during your illness—the mine of the yellow diamonds?'

But later, the old man would not utter a word about any of the things he had said in his delirium. Most of the time he would sit silently, wrapped in his own thoughts. In reply to Shankar's question he said, 'It's not that I haven't thought about it also. But do you have the courage to run after a will-o' the-wisp?'

Shankar said, 'Why don't you try me and find out whether or not I have the courage? If you want, I'll wire a message today to Mavo station and ask for a replacement.'

Alvarez thought for a while and said, 'All right, send them a telegram. But before that please understand that

those who go in search of gold or diamonds don't always find them. I used to know an eighty-year-old man—who never found anything. But every time he would say, "I think this time I know exactly where it is. This time I'll surely find it." All his life he wandered around the Australian desert and the African Veldt, prospecting.'

Ten days later, Shankar and Alvarez decided to travel to Kisumu and board a steamer on the Victoria-Nyanza Lake to go southwards towards Mwanza.

On the way, in a huge open grassland, Shankar was amazed to see thousands of zebras, giraffes and antelopes. He had never seen such a sight before.

The giraffes were not at all afraid of human beings. Maintaining a distance of about fifty yards, they kept watching the travellers.

Alvarez said, 'In Africa, to shoot a giraffe, you need a special license from the government. Everyone is not allowed to kill them. That's why giraffes are not afraid of humans.'

But the antelopes were easily frightened. There were about two or three hundred antelopes grazing in a herd. They raised their heads and had one look at the people—the next moment they had run to the far end of the grassland, galloping with their legs in the air.

The steamer left Kisumu. It was a British steamer. They were short of money so they travelled deck-class.

Some black women had boarded the steamer, carrying babies on their backs and poultry in their arms. Masai coolies were going home on leave. From Nairobi they had bought glass beads, cheap toys, mirrors and knives.

Disembarking from the steamer, they continued their journey. Mwanza, where they got off, was a port on Lake Victoria. Tabara was about three hundred miles from there. They would rest for a few days when they reached Tabara and then travel to the port of Uzizi on Lake Tanganyika.

On the way, Alvarez said that it was very dangerous to travel through Tanganyika. There is a species of fly; its bite causes sleeping sickness. Epidemics of sleeping sickness had almost destroyed the population of Tanganyika. There was also the danger of lions all along the way from Mwanza to Tabara. This part of Africa was really 'lion country'.

About ten miles from the city there was a small thatched hut. A European hunter had taken shelter there. He gave Alvarez a warm welcome. Seeing Shankar, he said, 'Where did you find him? Is he a Hindu? Is he your coolie?' Alvarez said, 'No, he is my son.'

The European was very surprised and asked 'How come?'

Alvarez recounted in detail the entire story of his illness and about Shankar's care and nursing. But he did not tell the man where they were going and what for.

The European smiled and said, 'That's good. His face tells me he is both brave and kind. The Hindus from the East Indies are certainly good people. I can never forget the lovely hospitality I received from a Sikh gentleman in Uganda. The night is drawing near, come and stay with me tonight. This is a Government Dak Bungalow. I only reached here late this afternoon, after travelling the whole day, like you.'

The gentleman had a gramophone. Later in the evening, after a meal of tinned tomato and sardines, as they were sitting on camp-chairs outside the bungalow and listening to one record after another, they heard the roar of lions. It was almost as if the lions were roaring with their heads to the ground—the earth was shaking with the sound.

The European said, 'The lions are a great menace in Tanganyika and they are extremely ferocious. Most of them are man-eaters. Once they have tasted human blood, they want nothing else.'

Shankar thought that was good news indeed! During the construction of the Uganda Railways he had had enough of lions.

The next morning they continued their journey. The hunter warned them, 'Be very careful, once the sun is up. The tsetse flies wake up with the sun—they must not come in contact with your skin.'

The paths were tunnel-like through the jungles of long elephant grass. Alvarez said, 'Be very careful, lions lurk in these jungles. Never fall behind.'

Alvarez had a gun. That gave Shankar some confidence. The other good thing was that Alvarez was what is known as a 'crack-shot'. His bullet rarely missed its mark. In spite of being in the company of such a remarkable hunter, Shankar did not feel completely safe. From his experience in Uganda, he knew that when a lion wants to take a man, he will do it with such suddenness that there wouldn't even be enough time to unstrap the leather rifle-case from the shoulders.

That day, an hour before dusk, they had to choose a place to rest for the night in the open grassland. Alvarez said, 'There is no village nearby. It is not safe to travel after dark.'

They made a small makeshift tent with two pieces of tarpaulin under a huge baobab tree. Shankar collected some twigs and branches, lit a fire, and got down to preparing the evening meal. A little later, tired after the toils of the day, they fell asleep.

Late at night, Alvarez called him, 'Shankar, wake up.' Shankar got up with a start.

Alvarez said, 'Some animal is hovering around the tent. Keep your gun ready . . .'

True enough, the breathing of an animal could be heard from beyond the thin tarpaulin curtain of the tent. In the dim light of the camp-fire, the huge baobab tree looked like a fearful giant. When Shankar tried to get off the bed with his gun, the old man forbade him.

The next instant, as the animal tried to push open the tent and enter, Alvarez fired twice from behind the tent curtain. Following the direction of the sound, Shankar too raised his gun but before he could press the trigger, Alvarez's rifle spoke once more. Then all was quiet.

They cautiously came out of the tent, torch in hand, and saw that a huge lion had entered, having pushed aside one part of the tent. It wasn't yet dead, but mortally wounded. It breathed its last with two more bullets.

Alvarez looked at the stars in the sky and said, 'Much of the night is still left. Let it be here. We must catch up with our sleep.'

Both of them went in and lay down. A little later, Shankar noticed with disbelief that Alvarez was snoring. Shankar couldn't sleep. About half an hour later Shankar felt that to keep company with Alvarez's snoring, all the lions of Tanganyika had started roaring in unison. What terrible roars they were! Shankar had heard lions roar a number of times earlier, but the tremendously frightening roars of that night, he would always remember. To make things worse, the roars were only yards away from the tent.

Alvarez woke up again and said, 'No, they won't allow you to sleep. It's the mate of the earlier lion. Be careful, Very dangerous animal.'

What a terrible night it was. The fire near the tent was dying and had only a faint glow. Beyond that it was pitch-dark. There was only the barrier of a thin sheet of tarpaulin and on the other side was a lioness whose mate had been killed. Roaring madly, it would sometimes go away, then come back again and at intervals circle the tent.

A little before dawn the lion went away. They too continued on their journey.

The Veldt

Fifteen days later Shankar and Alvarez boarded a steamer at the port of Uzizi and set out across Lake Tanganyika. On the other side of the lake they bought some necessities in a small town called Albertville. There was a Belgian government railway track from Albertville to Kabalo. From there, it was another three days' journey by steamer across the Congo river to Sanikini. Alighting at Sanikini, they had to leave the course of the Congo and travel south, venturing into a country full of unknown jungles and deserts.

Kabalo was a dirty place, just a settlement of a few Portuguese and Belgians of mixed blood.

No sooner had Shankar stepped outside the railway station, than a Portuguese came up to him and said, 'Hello, where are you going? You seem to be new here. Obviously you don't know me. My name is Albuqarque.'

Shankar looked back and saw that Alvarez was still inside the station.

The man looked as uncouth as he was ugly. But he seemed immensely strong. Almost seven feet tall, his muscles were so firm that each one could be counted.

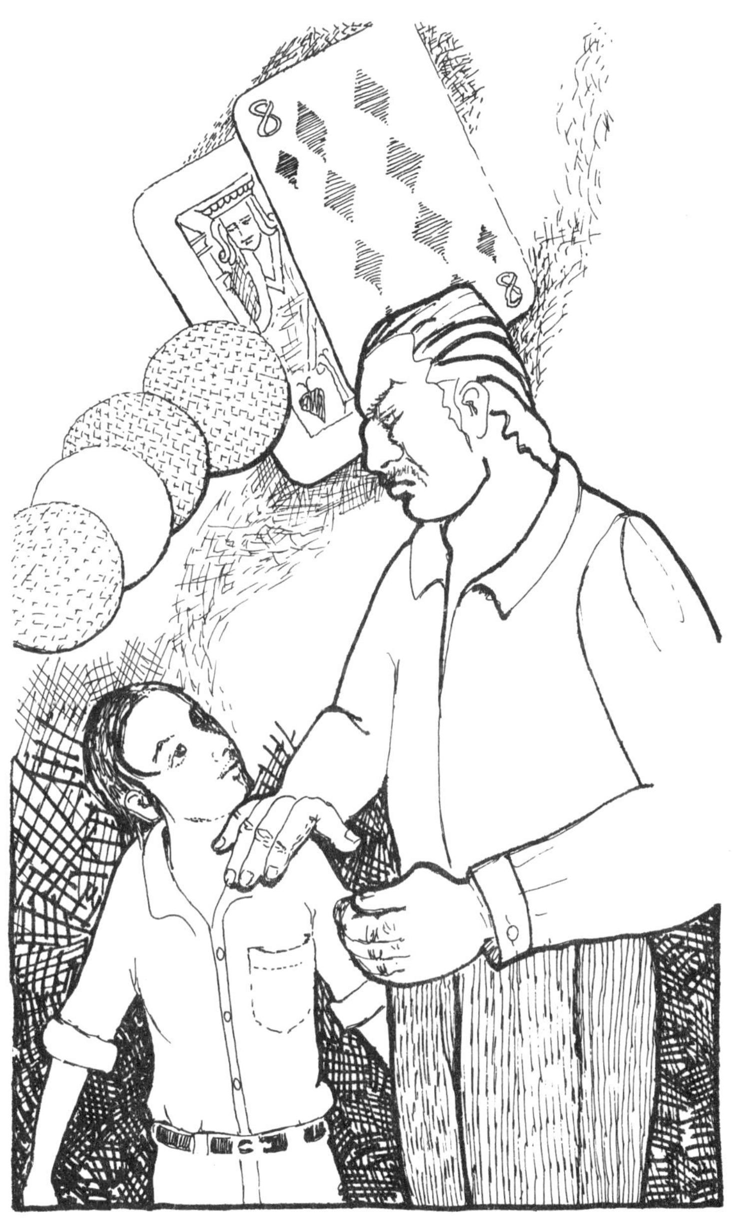

Shankar said, 'I am happy to meet you.' The man said, 'You look like a Blacky, probably from the East Indies. Come, you must play poker with me.'

The way the man spoke irritated Shankar. He said, 'I have no desire to play poker with you.' Shankar had also realised that, on the pretext of playing poker, the man wanted to rob him of everything. Poker was a form of gambling with cards. Shankar had heard of the game, but had never even seen it being played. While in Nairobi, he had learnt that wicked gamblers could ruin a person in the name of playing poker. It was just another form of robbery.

When he heard Shankar's reply the Portuguese rogue turned red with anger. His eyes looked as if they were going to spew fire. He came very close to Shankar and speaking hoarsely through clenched teeth told him, 'What? You nigger! What did you say? You seem a bit too cocky for an East Indian. For your future benefit please be informed that Albuqarque has killed dozens of Blackies like you with bullets from this revolver. You better listen to my rules. Every stranger that gets off at Kabalo station will either play poker with me or challenge me to a duel with a revolver.'

Shankar realised that if he got into a gunfight with this wicked rogue it would mean certain death. The hooligan was probably a crack-shot and a bully; and what was he? Till yesterday he was a harmless railway clerk. But if he chose not to fight and play poker, he would lose everything.

Shankar may have taken about half-a-minute to think this over and reply; but by that time the man had taken his gun out of the leather holster at his waist and, pointing the barrel at Shankar's stomach, said, 'Fight or poker.'

Shankar's blood suddenly reached boiling point. He was not going to be a coward and accept defeat from this crude animal. It didn't matter if he had to die. He was about to say 'fight' when a harsh stentorian voice said from behind, 'Watch out, you there! This bullet is going to blow your head off.'

Both of them were taken by surprise and turned to look. Alvarez was standing rigid holding his Winchester Repeater with the barrel firmly pointed at the head of the Portuguese rogue. Shankar saw his chance and quickly moved away from the direction of the barrel of Albuquarque's revolver. Alvarez said, 'You are challenging a mere boy to a duel? What a shame! By the time I have said three, you will drop your revolver, one . . . two . . . three . . .'

The revolver dropped from Albuqarque's unclenched hand.

Alvarez said, 'You were showing off how big and strong you were, because you found this young boy alone, right?'

Shankar in the meanwhile had picked up the revolver from the ground. Albuqarque seemed a little surprised. He had never expected Alvarez to be on Shankar's side. He smiled and said,

'Okay mate, don't get upset. I accept defeat. Now give me back my gun, young man. Don't worry, give it back. Come, let's shake hands. You're a mate too. Albuqarque doesn't nurse his anger. Come, my cabin is round the corner; let's have a glass of beer each.'

Alvarez was familiar with the temperament of his countrymen. He accepted the invitation and went to Albuqarque's cabin taking Shankar along with him. When Albuqarque heard that Shankar didn't drink beer, he offered him coffee. He talked of this and that and laughed and joked freely as if nothing had happened.

Shankar was truly attracted to this man. There were not many in this world who could completely forget the enmity and humiliation suffered moments ago and engage in genuine whole-hearted conversation with the same people who had humiliated him.

The next day they boarded a steamer from Kabalo to go south down the Congo. The scenery on both sides of the river filled Shankar's mind with joy.

He had never seen such unique landscapes of forests before. The parts of Africa that he had lived in till then abounded in huge stretches of open grassland, interspersed with a few acacia or yuca trees. But as the steamer progressed along the Congo, the two banks were increasingly covered with dense forests with many kinds of creepers and varieties of wild flowers. It was as if nature had run amok, and had lost herself in her own beauty and quiet abundance.

Shankar had a beauty-loving, sensitive mind. (After all, he was a boy from the villages of Bengal, not a hard-headed gold prospector like Diego Alvarez).

He was completely bewitched with this abundance of wild beauty and in the sunny afternoons and in the crimson evenings, his fascinated and enchanted mind would be lost in a web of dream-like wonderment.

Late at night, when everyone had gone to sleep, the wild mysterious nature of these forests would come alive under the canopy of a sky full of strange stars, with scores of different kinds of animal sounds floating down from the trees.

Sleep deserted Shankar's eyes. Captivated by this dreamland of beauty, he would stay awake all night, ignoring the chill in the air.

He could see the Saptarishi-mandal shining brightly. In another far corner of the sky the Saptarishi would also have risen above a small village in Bengal, and so would that small sliver of a waning moon in the dark night. He had travelled so far away from those familiar skies; who knew how far he still had to go!

Two days later, the steamer reached Sanikini. From there they went on foot. There weren't many forests there, but vast stretches of desolate grasslands and numberless small hills. Most of these hills were bare and treeless, although a few had shrubs like the euphorbia. But Shankar thought that this part of Africa looked beautiful. His mind was freed in these wide open spaces. The colours of the setting sun, the magic of the starry moonlit nights, transformed this into a land of fairies, every afternoon and evening.

Alvarez said, 'In these Veldts it's very easy to lose one's way, because everything looks the same.' The same day something happened which proved him right.

As the sun set across the lonely Veldt, they struck camp behind a small hill and lit a fire. Shankar went in search of water. He took Alvarez's gun with only two bullets in it. In half-an-hour, while he was still searching for water, daylight faded, and darkness slowly enveloped the entire grassland. Shankar could have sworn that he hadn't walked for more than half-an-hour. Looking around he felt an uncanny fear—as if there was some impending danger, and he must return to the tent. In the distance were a few hills, all looking alike in every direction, no land marks; all exactly the same.

After he had walked for perhaps another five or six minutes, Shankar began to feel he had lost his way. Then he remembered what Alvarez had said. Due to his lack of experience, he had not realised the seriousness of this danger. He walked and walked—at one moment he thought he should go straight ahead and at another moment he felt he should turn left or perhaps right. Why couldn't he see the tent-fire? Where was that small hill?

After walking for about two hours Shankar felt really frightened. He had realised, by that time, that he was completely lost and in deep trouble. He would have to spend the night in this desolate, lion-infested, unknown Rhodesian grassland—without food, and in this chilly winter, without blankets and without a fire. He didn't even have a box of matches.

To cut the story short, the next evening, almost twenty-four hours after he had lost his way, Alvarez found and rescued a delirious Shankar, half-dead with thirst, from under a euphorbia tree.

Alvarez said, 'Shankar, if I didn't find you today, the route that you had taken would have led you deeper and deeper into the desert and you would have died of thirst by afternoon tomorrow. A number of people like you have lost their lives in these Rhodesian Veldts. These are dangerous places. You are a novice still, so never again try to venture out of the tent on your own. If you don't know the rules and techniques of travelling in a desert, you'll surely die.'

Shankar said, 'Alvarez, you have saved my life twice. I'll never forget that.'

Alvarez replied, 'Young man, you are forgetting that earlier it was you who had saved my life. If you hadn't been there, my bones would have turned white in the Ugandan Savannahs, by now.'

After two months of trekking across the vast Veldts between Rhodesia and Angola, they at last caught sight of a huge mountain range in the distance, like clouds on the horizon. Alvarez consulted his map and said, 'That is our destination—the Richtersveld mountains. It must still be a good forty miles from here. In the open grasslands of Africa you can see things from very far.'

The place was full of baobab trees. Shankar had come to like these baobabs. From a distance they looked like Ashwathwa trees; but coming closer one could make out it was a baobab. They didn't give much shade, but were huge and gnarled, as if the tree had developed boils or tumours and looked rather like ugly ogres from the Arabian Nights. In those limitless Veldts they were strewn all over the place, far, near, everywhere.

One morning, while sitting in front of the tent-fire warming himself from the biting cold, Alvarez said, 'You see this Rhodesian Veldt; this place is full of diamonds, this is the country of diamond mines. You must have heard of the Kimberley mines. So many people have accidentally found diamonds here, both small and big. They still do.'

As soon as he had finished talking, he said, 'Who are they?'

Shankar was sitting across from him listening. He exclaimed, 'Who? Where?'

Alvarez's keen eyes were as unfailing as the bullets from his gun. A little later, Shankar could detect a few shadowy figures in the darkness, approaching them. Alvarez said, 'Shankar, go and get the gun; run for it and have it loaded.'

Shankar came out with the gun and saw Alvarez sitting and smoking calmly. The strange figures were still advancing towards them in the darkness. Soon they arrived and stood around the fire. Shankar saw that the visitors were dark and tall. Their hands were empty. They wore a piece of cloth around the loins, a strip of lion's mane around their necks and feathers as head-dress. They had well-built muscular bodies. In the light of the campfire they looked as if they were figures made of bronze.

Alvarez asked them in Zulu, 'What do you want?'

They talked amongst themselves for a while and then they all sat down. Alvarez said, 'Shankar, give them something to eat.'

Then lowering his voice he said, 'We are in grave danger, be very careful.'

Tins were opened and Shankar served everyone. Alvarez ate with them again although he had finished his supper before dark. Shankar guessed that Alvarez had some plan in mind, or probably local traditions required the host to join the guest for a meal.

Alvarez chatted in Zulu with the strangers while they ate. After a while, they finished their meal and left. Before they set off each one was presented with a cigarette.

After they left, Alvarez said, 'They belong to the Matabele tribe. They are exceptionally fierce and have fought a number of times with the British. They are not afraid of the Devil himself. They suspect that we have come to their country in search of diamond mines. The place where we are camping belongs to one of their tribal kings. No law of any civilised government will hold here. They'll just catch you and burn you alive. Let's get out of here.'

Shankar asked, 'But then why did you ask me to get the gun?'

Alvarez smiled and said, 'Look, I thought that if they were not satisfied with food alone or I guessed from their conversation that their intentions were not good, then we could have shot at them while they were eating. I sat down to eat with my revolver behind me. I would have finished all three. My name is Alvarez, there was a time when I too did not fear the Devil; even now I don't. My gun would have blown their brains out even before the food in their hands had reached their mouths.'

After travelling for another five or six days they entered a thick tropical jungle at the foothills of a great mountain range.

The place was as desolate as it was vast. Shankar was sure that if he lost his way this time, he wouldn't be able to find a way out in his lifetime. Alvarez too warned him, 'Shankar be very careful. Those who don't know how to travel in a forest could lose their way at every step. Lots of people have died helplessly, because everything looks the same here. There is no way of recognising and distinguishing one place from another. If you are not an experienced bush-man you'll face danger all the time. And remember, never step out without your gun. The jungles of Central Africa are not fashionable parks for tourists.'

The last remark was quite unnecessary. One look at the forests had made it clear to Shankar that they were no recreational parks! Instead he asked, 'How far do you think your yellow diamond mine would be from here? The map shows that those are the Richtersveld mountains.'

Alvarez smiled and said, 'I told you, you are a novice. These are really the outer ridges of the main Richtersveld. There are many ridges like this. The entire range is so huge that even if you travelled for seventy miles to the east and another hundred or hundred and fifty miles to the west, you would not come to the end of these mountains or this jungle. At its narrowest point, the range is forty miles wide. Altogether these mountains and forests of the Richtersveld cover eight to nine thousand square miles. To find the particular spot which I had last seen seven or eight years ago amidst this huge uncharted region is no child's play, young man.'

Shankar said, 'Our rations are over too. We have to start hunting for food, otherwise we'll have to live on fresh air.'

Alvarez remarked, 'Don't worry. Can't you see the swarms of baboons in the trees? If we can't find anything else, we can have a lovely breakfast of roasted baboon limbs and coffee. Let's not go any further today. Let us pitch tent here and rest.'

They put up their tent under a large tree and lit a fire. Shankar cooked. When they had finished their supper and sat down in front of the fire, there was still some daylight left.

Alvarez lit his pipe and smoking his strong roasted tobacco said, 'You know Shankar, in these unexplored forests of Africa, there are many animals about which science still has no clue. Very few civilised people have come here. The Okapi was first seen only in 1900. There is a species of wild boar that are three times as large as the common wild boar. In 1888, Moses Cowley, a great explorer and hunter, first saw these huge boars in the Lualabu jungles of the Belgian Congo. He hunted one with great difficulty and presented the carcass to the Museum of Natural History in New York. Have you heard of the famous Rhodesian Monster?'

Shankar said, 'No, what is it?'

Alvarez continued, 'Listen to me then. Towards the northern boundaries of Rhodesia, there are huge swamps. Quite a few of the savage Zulus who inhabit that area have reported sightings of a very strange animal from time to time. They say its head is like a crocodile's, it has horns like the rhino, the neck is long and scaly like that of a python, the body is that of a hippo and the tail again like a crocodile's. This huge animal is reputed to be extremely ferocious. It has never been seen out of the water and on dry land. But it is difficult to believe the accounts and descriptions of these illiterate locals.

In 1880, a prospector called James Martin had roamed these parts for a long time in search of gold. Martin was previously the aide-de-camp of General Mathews; in addition, he was a competent geologist and zoologist. In his diary he has mentioned that in those remote and unknown parts of Rhodesia he saw this creature from a distance. He too had said that, in shape and size, the animal looked reptilian and was huge like the dinosaurs of prehistory. But he had only seen this strange beast rather indistinctly in the morning fog above the swamps near Lake Kovirando, and so could not be very certain about it. The moment his Zulu coolies heard the screams of the creature, which was like the neighing of a horse, they started running pell-mell saying, "Sahib run for life, Dingonek! Dingonek!" Dingonek was the Zulu name for this beast. It is very rarely seen; hardly once in two or three years. But it has such a fearsome reputation that any sighting of this creature strikes terror throughout the country. Mr. Martin had written that he had fired two successive rounds of his .303 rifle at the animal. But the creature was not within effective range, and probably dived into the water on hearing the sound of the rifle.'

Shankar said, 'How do you know all this? Was Martin's diary published?'

'No, a long time ago, *The Bulwaye Chronicle* published an article about this incident. I had then just arrived in this country. The description of the beast was of great interest to me because I was prospecting in Rhodesia in those days. I preserved the paper carefully for many years. Then I lost it somewhere. The paper had named the beast—the Rhodesian Monster.'

Shankar said, 'Did you ever see any unknown animal?'

As soon as he asked this question, something strange happened.

The evening darkness had deepened by then. In the shadows Shankar had an uneasy feeling, although he could have been mistaken. He felt as if the intrepid and fearless Alvarez, the shrewd crack-shot Alvarez seemed to startle suddenly at this question; and what was even more amazing, the next moment he seemed to tremble.

Simultaneously Alvarez, unconscious of himself, looked at the thick, desolate forests and the mysterious impassable mountains all around, but said nothing. As if, coming to these forests and mountains after so long, he had remembered some incident from the past—an unpleasant and unwelcome memory.

Alvarez was frightened!

Impossible! Alvarez, afraid? Shankar couldn't believe it! But unknown to him, that fear found a place in his mind too. It was as if these totally unknown and strangely mysterious forests and that huge mountain had hidden some deep secret for aeons. The brave and the fearless could come—but they had to wager their very lives to find those secrets.

The Richtersveld mountains are not like the divine Himalayas of India, Lords of the Mountains. Like the Masais, the Zulus, the Matabeles and other ancient tribes of this country, the soul of the mountain is cruel and hungry for human flesh. It will spare no one.

Across the Richtersveld Range

A couple of days passed. They went deeper and deeper into the forest. All along the way, the track was uneven. In places there were stretches of tall, rough grass. Water was scarce. Even when they came across a stream, Alvarez would not permit Shankar to even touch the water. The water flowing down the streams seemed clear as crystal, cool and tempting. It was extremely difficult for a thirsty person to resist that water. But Alvarez would rather have him sip cold tea, than allow him to drink the water. Cold tea could never quench thirst. At one place the grass grew very thick; the fog above was equally dense. But as the sun came higher up the fog at ground level disappeared quite suddenly. Looking up, Shankar saw that a steep mountain wall was blocking their way. How high it was, he couldn't say, because of the fog and clouds that completely covered the upper regions.

Alvarez said, 'That's the main Richtersveld range.'

Shankar asked, 'Do we have to cross that?'

Alvarez replied, 'If it is necessary; because the last time Jim and I came from the south right up to the foothills of the mountain, but did not cross the main range. The

Mithila M.

stream beside which we discovered the yellow diamonds flowed from east to west. Now we are travelling from north to south. So if we don't cross the range and go over to the other side, how can we ever find the river?'

Shankar said, 'But look at the thick fog today, wouldn't it be better to wait for a while? Let the sun come up a little higher.'

They pitched the tent and had their meal. But even later, the fog didn't clear much. Shankar fell asleep in the tent. When he woke up, it was almost dusk. Wiping his eyes, Shankar came out of the tent, and found Alvarez sitting with the map unfolded in front of him and a troubled look on his face. When he saw Shankar, he said,

'Shankar, we still have a great deal of trouble ahead. Just look up and see.'

Shankar looked up and beheld a most daunting sight. The fog had lifted by then and in front of him stood the main branch of the massive Richtersveld mountain range, ascending in enormous steps, until it seemed to hit the sky. Although the middle-level of this mountain was covered with clusters of lightning-filled clouds, the high peaks were bathed in the light of the setting sun and standing high in the blue firmament, like temples of gold in the abode of gods.

But the section of the mountain that lay straight ahead seemed extremely difficult to climb—sheer vertical peaks without any sign of a gradual slope.

Alvarez said, 'It would be impossible to climb this mountain from this side, Shankar, you must have realised that by now. Let's follow the valley westward. Whenever and wherever we find a slope and a valley, we will try and cross the hills from there. But to find such a pass on this one hundred and fifty mile long range, may take us more than a month.'

However, only five or six days later, they found a place where the mountain had a gentle slope along its side and from where it was possible to start their ascent.

The next morning, they started their climb very early. By Shankar's watch the time was then six-thirty. But by about eight-thirty he felt he couldn't go any further. The place they had chosen for their ascent had an extremely steep gradient, rising six thousand feet within a distance of four miles. The climb proved to be extremely strenuous. Besides, the higher they climbed, the thicker the jungle got, so it became quite dark under the canopy of trees. It was midday, and the sun was blazing above; but there was no light inside the jungle. Even the sky couldn't be seen!

There was no such thing as a track. All they could see were tree-trunks going up the slope in steps, right up to the sky. It was a mystery from where the water was coming; but the rocks underfoot were wet and slippery and covered with moss. If by chance a foot slipped, one would roll hundreds of feet down and hit the sharp-edged rocks in the valley below.

Neither Shankar or Alvarez spoke. Both were extremely tired. They panted and puffed all the time. Shankar felt the pain and exertion much more. After all he had grown up in the plains of Bengal; he had no experience in climbing mountains.

Shankar kept hoping Alvarez would give the signal to stop and rest. He just couldn't climb any further, but even if he had to die, he wouldn't tell Alvarez that he could not carry on. If he did Alvarez would think that these people from India were totally useless. In those vast, terrible mountains and forests he was representing India—he would not let himself do anything that would belittle his motherland.

It was a beautiful forest, a land of fairies. Here and there were little streams flowing down the slopes from great heights to the valley below. In the branches of trees, parrots of many colors were flying around in a dazzling display. The clumps of tall grass were topped with bunches of white blossoms; and hanging from the branches or clinging to the trunks of trees, were exotic orchids.

Suddenly Shankar noticed a rather strange sight among the branches of the big trees. Who were those people with long flowing beards and drooping moustaches sitting on the branches like dwarf sages? They were all sitting quietly and somberly with sage-like expressions. What was happening?

Alvarez said, 'Those are the female colobus monkeys. The males have neither beards nor moustaches. But the females grow long beards and whiskers, and they always have a grave look about them. Didn't you notice?'

Shankar burst out laughing watching their antics.

Under their feet, they felt neither soil nor rock. They were walking on a floor of just rotten leaves and decaying twigs and branches. In such forests, fallen leaves and branches accumulate and rot over centuries! On top of it all was a thick layer of moss, fungus and toad-stools; then again a fresh layer of dead leaves and branches and even tree-trunks. At places like this, the carpet of decaying vegetation could be sixty or seventy feet deep.

Alvarez taught him that he should step very carefully. There were spots where a person could simply sink into those piles of rotting leaves, like falling into an old well, and die of suffocation.

Shankar said 'The jungle is becoming more and more dense. We can't continue to climb unless we start cutting down the branches to make a path.'

The elephant grass was tall, broad and razor-sharp, like the two-edged broad swords of the Romans.

Manoeuvering through these, neither of them could believe they were safe, especially when they couldn't see anything even a couple of feet ahead. Anything could happen; they could face danger at any moment. There could be leopards, lions, poisonous snakes.

Shankar noticed that from time to time he could hear a sound like that of the bongo or the drum from some distance. 'Are one of the savage tribes beating their drums?' he asked Alvarez.

Alvarez said 'They are not drums. Large baboons or apes sometimes make that kind of sound when they beat their breasts. Where would you find human beings in this wild place?'

Shankar said, 'But you told me that there are no gorillas in these forests.'

Alvarez answered, 'Gorillas are unlikely. In the whole of Africa, gorillas are found only in parts of the Belgian Congo, in the Rwenzori Alps or in the mountains of the Virunga volcano. That kind of sound can also be made by other species of large apes.'

They had climbed about four and a half thousand feet, and pitched the tent there for the night. In these huge tropical jungles, the sounds at night could be so strange and eerie, that Shankar could not close his eyes the entire night. It wasn't just fear; it was a mixture of apprehension and awe.

How many different kinds of sounds he could hear—the hyena's howl, the shrill cries of the colobus monkeys, the sound of apes beating their breasts, the roar of lions. In that enormous natural zoo no one seemed to sleep at night. The entire forest came suddenly alive in the middle of the night.

A few years before, a big circus party had come to Shankar's village and camped in the field near the school boarding-house. The animals made so much noise all through the night that the boys in the hostel could hardly sleep. Those memories came back to Shankar. But when a herd of wild elephants started trumpeting from somewhere quite close, Shankar got a terrible fright. He woke Alvarez who reassured him, 'There is a fire burning outside the tent. Don't worry they won't come near us.'

Thc next morning there was more climbing up the mountain. They climbed and climbed through miles and miles of jungles of wild bamboo, clumps of wild ginger. At one place a huge herd of wild elephants passed within fifty yards from them through the bamboo jungle to their left, noisily breaking off the young shoots and munching them on their way.

At a height of five thousand feet there was a veritable show of wild flowers—the bright red irythrina blooming on enormous trees, the blossoming ipomia looking very much like the wild kalmi plant of Bengal—though the colour was not as dark a purple. The air around here was heavy with the smell of the white veronica; and here and there were wild coffee plants abloom with coffee flowers; and of course the colourful begonia. It was a forest of flowers in the realm of clouds. All around, small clusters of clouds hung in the topmost branches of the trees like huge white balloons; or sometimes the clouds would come lower and moisten the veronica shrubs.

At a height of over seven and a half thousand feet the character of the forest changed completely. They took another two days to reach that level. The climb was back-breaking. The face of the forest here was fascinatingly different—the trunks and the branches of every tree were covered with thick moss; clumps of moss were hanging from the branches. The moss was so thick and so long that in places it would almost touch the ground, swinging in the breeze. No sunlight reached them. Below the branches, it was dusk all the time; and all around there reigned an eerie silence—there was not even the sound of the wind blowing. No birds sang in that forest, no human voices, not even the sound of animal life. It was as if they had arrived in a dark underworld amidst long-haired ghosts.

That afternoon when Alvarez gave orders to camp and rest, Shankar had a peculiar feeling as he sipped his coffee outside his tent. He suddenly realised that these forests had been there since the very beginning of life on earth, when plants and vegetation were still in a state of evolution. They were from a time when huge dinosaurs roamed the earth, in the marshes and in thick jungles. By some magic he had been transported to that primordial world.

As evening descended, the entire forest was enveloped in thick darkness. They had built a fire outside the tent—beyond the meagre light thrown by the flames, they could see nothing. Shankar was overwhelmed by the intense stillness of the forest. Where were the night-sounds of the forest? Why was everything steeped in silence? Alvarez, studying the map with a grave expression, said 'Listen Shankar, I have been thinking. We have climbed eight thousand feet, but still we haven't found the pass through which we can cross the range to the other side. How much more can we climb? The saddle is nowhere near this part of the mountain.'

It was not as if the thought hadn't occurred to Shankar. The same day he had tried, several times, to look through the field glasses as he climbed, but every time thick fog or heavy clouds blocked his vision. If they couldn't find the pass through this part of the mountain, they would have to go all the way down and climb up again. That would be a real disaster.

He said, 'What does the map say?'

Alvarez seemed to have lost confidence in the map. He said, 'This map is not a detailed one. Who has ever climbed this mountain that you'll get a proper map?

What you see here is a map prepared by Sir Phillipo de Phillipi. He earned great fame by climbing the Ferdinando Po peak in Portuguese West Africa. A few years ago he joined an expedition led by the famous mountaineer and explorer, the Duke of Abruzzi. But he never climbed the Richtersveld. The contours of the hills drawn in this map don't appear to be accurate at all. I am really confused.'

Suddenly Shankar said, 'What's that?'

There was a faint noise outside the tent, and the next moment a sound like a painful cough, as if some one suffering from tuberculosis was coughing with great difficulty. Once . . . twice . . . then the sound stopped. But the sound was not human, Shankar thought, as soon as he heard it.

He was just about to go out of the tent, rifle in hand, when Alvarez got up and caught him by the hand and sat him down. Surprised, Shankar said, 'Why, what was that sound?' He looked at Alvarez and saw that his face had gone pale with fear. Just from hearing that sound?

At that moment, beyond the fire outside the tent, in the darkness, a heavy but light-footed animal moved through the jungle.

They were both very silent for a few moments. Then, Alvarez said, 'Put more logs into the fire. Check if both guns are loaded.' Looking at his face Shankar thought the better of asking more questions.

The night passed.

The next morning Shankar woke up early. He went a little distance from the tent to get some firewood to make coffee. Suddenly he noticed a footprint on the wet ground. It was at least eleven inches in length but had only three toes. All three toes had left deep imprints. He followed the footprints for quite a distance.

Shankar remembered Alvarez's story of Jim Carter's death—the three-toed footprints of that terrible and unknown animal at the entrance of the cave. The story told by the chief of the Kaffir village.

He also remembered Alvarez's terrified look of the previous night. The only other day that he had seen Alvarez so frightened was the first day they had pitched their tent at the foot of the mountain.

Bunip! The Kaffir chief's story of the dreaded Bunip! The terror of the Richtersveld mountains and forests. Such is the fear of this dreaded beast that let alone savage men, even savage animals do not venture into these jungles above eight thousand feet. Even the fearless Alvarez had gone ashen with fear, just hearing the sound of the animal's voice. Perhaps he had heard that sound before.

Alvarez woke up a little late that morning. After he had breakfast and coffee, he was back to his normal self—the intrepid Alvarez—who fears neither man nor devil. Shankar purposely didn't show those footprints to Alvarez, just in case he changed his mind and said 'We haven't found the saddle yet. Let's go down.'

That morning, there were dark clouds and a heavy shower. Along the slopes of the mountain the rainwater flowed down like a thousand waterfalls. The mountain and the forests overwhelmed one's senses. At every thousand feet the tops of the trees just below looked as if they were jungles in the plains. It seemed that they had hardly climbed at all!

It didn't stop raining that morning. After waiting till ten o'clock, Alvarez gave orders to strike tent. Shankar hadn't expected this. He now saw another side to the character of his white companion. He was thinking, 'Why go out in this rain? What difference would one day make? What is the point of walking and getting drenched?'

Braving the endless downpour and cutting through the dense forest, they climbed all through the day. Going up, and up—Shankar could hardly walk. Their clothes, their provisions, their tent, everything was completely drenched—there wasn't even a dry handkerchief left. Shankar felt a great weariness—physical and mental—come over him.

Towards the evening, when the entire mountain and the forests became terrifyingly dark and forbidding under the double cover of the clouds and the night, some very disturbing thoughts passed through Shankar's mind.

In this strange country, across the tops of uncharted mountains covered with dense forests full of blood-thirsty beasts, why was he running towards some undiscovered diamond mine or perhaps towards some unknown death? Who was Alvarez? Why did he listen to him and come this far? He had no need of diamonds. The straw-thatched huts of his village in Bengal, the shady and sleepy village-paths, the little stream, the familiar chirping of birds—they all seemed so far away—like some unreal dream. No diamond mine of Africa was more precious than that!

But his mood changed late at night, when the moon came up in the cloudless sky. That unearthly moonlit night beggared description! Shankar wasn't in this world anymore, there was no land called Bengal. Everything became a dream, except that beautiful night. He didn't want to go back anywhere, he had no need for diamonds or for wealth. He had become the inhabitant of this lotus-white realm of the gods—far far above this earth. No human had ever set his eyes on the beauty that surrounded him—no one had felt that deep silence. Far away from human habitation, the great Richtersveld mountains and its forests, with the stillness of the night around them, sat on the lap of clouds as if in deep meditation, lost in themselves. It was a rare sight and rarer was the chance to be part of it.

That night he woke up with a start, hearing Alvarez call out, 'Shankar, Shankar, get up. Take the gun.'

'What happened?'

Then he listened carefully—it was as if someone or something was walking around the tent, its loud breathing could be heard distinctly. The moon was near the horizon, so the outside was mostly dark. The faint moonlight shone on the high branches of trees, nothing could be seen clearly. The fire near the tent was still alive, but too weak to cast its brightness beyond a few feet. It wasn't of much help.

Suddenly there was a crashing noise—as if a large animal was running away breaking through the undergrowth. The beast seemed to have understood that the people in the tent had woken up and that it had lost the advantage of a surprise attack.

Whatever beast it was, it was intelligent and could think on its own.

Alvarez went out of the tent, rifle and torch in hand. Shankar followed him. In the light of the torch they could see that outside the north-east corner of the tent, the entire undergrowth was flattened as if a steam-roller had gone over it. Alvarez raised his rifle and fired twice in that direction.

There was no response from any direction.

As they came back to the tent, they both noticed footprints near the tent door and right next to the campfire. The impression of the three toes was distinct on the wet ground.

It clearly proved that the beast was not afraid of fire.

Shankar realised that, if they didn't wake up, that unknown terror would not have hesitated to enter the tent. He thought the better of imagining what would have happened next.

Alvarez said, 'Shankar, you better sleep the rest of the night, I'll stay awake.'

Shankar said, 'No, better you sleep Alvarez.'

Alvarez smiled and said, 'Don't be ridiculous. You wouldn't achieve anything staying awake, Shankar. Go to sleep, see there's lightning in the distance, it's going to rain again. The night is almost over. So grab a little sleep. I'll make myself some coffee.'

With the break of dawn came a heavy downpour accompanied by lightning and thunder. It rained the whole day, without respite. Shankar felt it was the rain to end the world. The god of destruction had let loose this terrible downpour to flood the entire earth. Even the indomitable Alvarez could not bring himself to give orders to strike tent and move.

It was about five in the evening when the rain finally stopped. It would have been better if it had continued to raïn. Because, no sooner had it stopped raining, than Alvarez gave orders to move. The typical Bengali, Shankar thought why start at this late hour? What difference would this make—how much time would they gain? But to Alvarez—day, night, rain, sun, moonlight, darkness—everything was the same. That night, as the two of them climbed up through the wet forests, in the light of the moon streaming through the scattered clouds, Alvarez suddenly shouted, 'Shankar! Wait! Look there . . .'

Alvarez was looking through his field glasses towards the peak on the left. Shankar took the glasses from him and looked in that direction. Yes, there was a flat valley cutting across. It wasn't too far also, perhaps a couple of miles to their left.

Alvarez was smiling, and said 'Can you see the saddle? Let's not stop. We'll make it to the saddle tonight and pitch tent there.' Shankar was hardly able to walk. What trouble he had brought upon himself teaming up with this irrepressible Portuguese, in search of diamonds! Shankar knew that in an expedition he must not question the decisions of the leader. Here Alvarez was the leader—his orders could not be disobeyed. It was an unwritten law in all expeditions throughout history, and Shankar would obey it.

Walking continuously, they finally reached the saddle at sunrise. By that time, Shankar had no energy left to move another step!

The saddle was not less than three miles in width. It would suddenly rise steeply a couple of hundred feet and then, within a mile, go sharply down four or five hundred feet. So it was a difficult climb. Wherever it was flat the valley was thickly forested with huge trees—erythriana, penciana, soap-nut, bamboo and wild ginger. Colourful, exotic orchids hung from the branches. The place was full of baboons and colobus monkeys.

They climbed down the saddle slope for the next two days, until they reached the valley on the other side of the main Richtersveld range. Shankar felt that the forest on this side was even more dense and exotic. The wet winds rising from the Atlantic hit the Cameroon mountains in West Africa, and the rest are arrested by the southern ledge of the massive Richtersveld mountains. So, rainfall here was in plenty; the vegetation, similarly, was abundant.

They searched that forested valley for about two weeks, and yet they could not find the mountain stream that Alvarez had marked in the map. They did come across a couple of small streams, but at each place Alvarez shook his head and said, 'No, not this one.'

Shankar said to him, 'Why don't you look at your map carefully?' It seemed that Alvarez's map was not quite accurate.

Alvarez said, 'What's the point in looking at the map? The place is deeply etched in my mind. Once I am able to set my eyes on that valley and that river, I'll recognise it immediately. This is not the valley I am looking for.'

And so they continued the search!

A month passed. The West African rainy season started in early March. What a terrible bout of rain it was. Shankar had a taste of it when they were crossing the Richtersveld. The valley was almost washed away by huge streams coming down the mountains. There was hardly a dry place where they could pitch their tent. One night, a little stream near their tent suddenly ballooned into a huge river of water, and almost washed them away with their tent. They were saved in the nick of time, thanks to Alvarez being a light and wary sleeper.

If days passed, time lingered. Shankar got into serious trouble in the jungle one day. The trouble was of a very peculiar nature.

That day Alvarez was cleaning his rifle inside the tent, after which he was to cook the day's meal. Shankar went out gun in hand to look for game.

Alvarez warned him that he should move very carefully in the forest and his gun should be ready at all times. Another very valuable piece of advice he gave Shankar was, 'Always wear the compass on your right wrist and, whichever way you go, keep marking the trees or branches in such a way that you can retrace your steps by finding those marked trees on your way back. Otherwise you are bound to get into trouble.'

That day Shankar went deep into the jungles looking for Springbok deer. He had set out early in the morning and after a while felt rather tired walking around. He sat down under a large tree to rest.

All around the tree was a great variety of vegetation. He noticed specifically that all the trees were covered by a large creeper. These creepers were so thick and dense that one could hardly see the trunks of the trees. Nearby, there were thick clusters of maripasa lily, growing on the banks of a marsh.

After a while, Shankar began to feel uncomfortable. He could not exactly name the nature of his discomfort—but all the same didn't feel like getting up either. He was tired and the place felt like a nice spot to rest.

But what was happening to him? Why was he feeling totally drained of energy? Was he developing a malarial fever?

To get rid of the lethargy, he searched his pockets, found a cheroot and lit it. There was some kind of a sweet smell wafting around. Shankar quite liked the fragrance. A little later, when he tried to pick up the box of matches lying on the ground and put it in his pocket, he felt as if the hand was not his, but someone else's. He couldn't get himself to move it. Gradually his entire body began to be overcome by a kind of a pleasant exhaustion. What was the point in roaming around for nothing; it was like running after a ghost. What could be better than to spend time in lazy dreams amidst the cool sequestered shades of this forest?

At one point he thought—'I better get up and go back to the tent otherwise some major calamity might take place.' He even tried to get up once, but in the next instant he was overcome by a body-and-mind-sapping exhaustion. No, it was not even exhaustion, but some kind of a pleasant stupor, as if he was drunk. The world seemed distant and trivial. This heady state was gradually paralysing his entire body.

Shankar finally lay down with his head on the roots of the tree. Around him, the scenery was not quite distinct amidst intermittent patches of light and shade under the huge silk-cotton trees. From somewhere close by came the loud hooting of wild owls, which slowly grew more and more faint. Shankar didn't know what happened to him after that.

When Alvarez, after searching for a long time, found him at last, it was almost evening and he was unconscious. At first Alvarez thought Shankar had been bitten by a snake. But when he examined the body he found no sign of a snake bite. Suddenly, he noticed the creepers above and, being an experienced traveller, took no time to guess what had happened. These creepers were deadly poisonous and their sap was used by the tribes of that area to tip their arrows. The air was heavy with its fragrance, and inhaling too much of that air could cause paralysis, even death.

Back in the tent Shankar had to be in bed for two or three days. His whole body had swollen up like a balloon. He felt as if his head was going to burst and his throat was dry as firewood. Alvarez said, 'If you had spent the night there, it would have been difficult to save you in the morning.'

One day, under the flowing waters of a small waterfall, Shankar saw something yellow. Alvarez was an expert prospector. He soon found some grains of gold, after washing away the sand. But he didn't seem too excited about the find. The percentage of gold was so little that it wouldn't be worth the labour of recovering it—a tonne of sand would hardly yield three ounces of gold.

Shankar said, 'But why waste time, let's take whatever we can get. Even three ounces of gold will get good money.'

What Shankar thought was novel and exciting, was of no value to an experienced prospector like Alvarez. Besides, Shankar's idea of 'labour' was quite different from Alvarez's definition of it. Ultimately, Shankar just had to give up the idea.

In the meanwhile, they combed the jungle for about a month. They would pitch tent at a spot for a couple of days, look around, and then move to another. One day they had pitched tent at a new place. Shankar went out, gun in hand. When he came back to the tent in the evening with a couple of birds in his bag, he found Alvarez sitting and smoking a cheroot. Alvarez looked anxious and worried.

Shankar said, 'Alvarez, I tell you, since you yourself cannot find the place, let's go back.'

Alvarez said 'The river couldn't have just vanished into thin air. It's here somewhere, in some corner of this mountain, these forests.'

'Then why haven't we found it?'

'Because we are not searching the right way.'

'What are you saying Alvarez? We have been scouring this jungle for six months. How much better can one search?'

Alvarez became very grave and said 'You know what the problem is, Shankar? I haven't told you yet, because I was afraid you would get very discouraged, perhaps even frightened. Well, let me show you something. Come with me.'

Shankar followed him, full of curiosity and interest. What was the matter?

Alvarez walked for some distance, stopped near a tree and said, 'Shankar, we have pitched tent here only today, right?'

Shankar was very surprised and said 'What are you trying to say? Of course, we have come here only today.'

'Right then, come and take a close look at the trunk of this tree.'

Shankar looked and saw that someone had cut the soft bark with a knife and carved the letters D.A. But the etching was not recent, at least a month old!

Shankar didn't quite understand and kept looking at Alvarez. Alvarez said, 'You didn't get it? I had written my initials on this tree a month ago. I was becoming a little suspicious. You can't make out, because for you all forests are the same. Now do you understand? We have been going round in circles in this forest. When you fall into a trap like this, it's very difficult to get out.'

Shankar understood at last. He said, 'You mean, we had been right here a month ago?'

'Exactly. In a large forest or desert, this kind of danger is lurking all the time. These are called 'death circles'. I suspected almost a month ago that we have been trapped in a death circle. I etched my name on that tree only to confirm my misgivings. I suddenly noticed it today when I was strolling around.'

Shankar said, 'What happened to our compass? How could we be going around in circles everyday, with a compass in hand?'

Alvarez said, 'I think our compass has stopped working. You remember that terrible bout of thunder and lightning when we were crossing the Richtersveld? Perhaps that was when the compass lost its magnetic bearings.'

'That means our compass is now useless.'

'That's what I think.'

Shankar thought it was indeed a nice situation to be in. They had an inaccurate map and a useless compass; they were trapped in the whirls of a deathly circle in the depths of an impenetrable jungle. Not a soul anywhere, they had no food and had almost run out of water. They could not take the risk of drinking from the forest streams. The only thing that confronted them was the terrifying thought of unforeseen death. Jim Carter had met his death looking for diamonds in these cursed jungles. It didn't seem that the place would do anyone any good.

But Alvarez was not the type to give up so easily. The next day they set off again through the forest. Shankar could see no beginning nor end to the jungle. Whatever little he could make out, was lost from the moment he heard that they were in the death circle. He had simply lost all sense of direction.

Three days later, they arrived at a place where a branch of the Richtersveld met the main range at right angles, towards the north. It was at least four thousand feet high. Further to the west, another very high peak played hide-and-seek with the clouds. The valley between the two mountains was at least three miles wide and densely forested.

In these forests, the vegetation seemed to have three or four distinct layers. On the top there were only parasites and moss, in the middle were trees of various sizes and at the bottom, near the ground, were shrubs and small plants. Hardly any sunlight could penetrate that triple layer.

Alvarez suggested that they pitch tent at the edge of this forest. In the evening, while having coffee, they started discussing what they should do next. They had no food left, the sugar was finished long ago, and the coffee too was going to run out in a few days. A little flour remained—but nothing else. They lived mainly on the flesh of birds and animals. But since they didn't have an ammunition factory with them, how long could they hope to survive by hunting?

While talking, Shankar kept looking at the distant peak playing hide-and-seek with the clouds. For a short spell, the clouds disappeared altogether. The peak was a strange sight—it was as if someone had bitten off a side of the top of an ice cream.

Alvarez said, 'From here Bulwaye and Salisbury are about four to five hundred miles towards the south-east. In between, there lies two hundred miles of desert. To the west, the sea is certainly closer, around three hundred miles away, but Portuguese West Africa is full of the most dense and dangerous forests. So let's not talk of that. The only course of action left to us is that either you or I go to Salisbury or Bulwaye, and get some more food and ammunition. We need a compass too.'

It was in a truly auspicious moment that Shankar heard Alvarez say this. What providence does for men;

how many understand and appreciate that? By sheer luck Shankar heard the names of the two towns Salisbury and Bulwaye, their general direction and approximate distance. Later, how many times he would thank Alvarez for telling him the names of these two cities!

They didn't talk much longer that evening. They were tired and went to sleep early.

The Bed of the Fire God

Shankar woke up in the middle of the night. There was a sound coming from the depths of the forest. Something was happening out there in the jungle. Alvarez too had woken up. Both listened with their ears perked up. What was going on out there? Shankar was about to hurry out of the tent with a lighted torch. Alvarez stopped him. He said, 'Never venture out of the tent into the jungle at night, in a hurry. I have warned you many times. And why are you going out without a gun?'

Outside the tent, it was pitch dark. Shining their torches out, they saw wild animals running for their lives, breaking through the thick undergrowth. They were fleeing the western part of the forest, frenzied and frightened, towards the eastern hills—hyenas, baboons, wild buffaloes. Two cheetahs almost brushed past them. More were coming, in packs and herds. Adult male and female colobus monkeys were running, carrying their babies. All seemed to be fleeing some imminent catastrophe. Together with all this was a strange sound—it was the sound of suppressed thunder, or as if a thousand drums were being beaten all together!

What was the matter? Alvarez and Shankar looked at each other. Both were at a loss. Alvarez said, 'Shankar, stoke up the fire, or else these wild beasts will go right over the tent, breaking and trampling it, with us inside.'

The number of animals fleeing kept increasing. Even the birds were flying over them, leaving their nests behind. A huge herd of Springboks passed within a few yards of their tent. But they were so awestruck with what was happening that they forgot to raise their guns and fire even at that close range. They had never seen a sight like that in their lives!

Shankar was just going to ask something of Alvarez—when apocalypse struck, or that is what Shankar thought. The entire earth shook and trembled with such violence that they both toppled to the ground. Simultaneously, it seemed a thousand peals of thunder burst together. The ground was ripped apart and the sky seemed to explode.

Alvarez, while attempting to get on to his feet, said, 'Earthquake!'

But at the next instant they were taken by complete surprise. The thick darkness of the night had given way to a brilliant light as if fifty thousand electric lights had been lit. Where did this light come from?

Then their eyes fell on the distant peak of the mountain. A huge display of fireworks seemed to have started there. The entire horizon was red with the glow of that massive holocaust. Clouds, red like the light of fire, were gorging out of the peak rising two or three thousand feet above the mountain. And together with that, the suffocating stench of burning sulphur permeated the air all around!

Alvarez stared and cried out in fear and awe, 'Volcano! Santa Anna Grazia Cordoba!'

What a terrifyingly beautiful sight it was! For a while neither of them could turn their eyes away from that sight. Shankar felt as if a million fireworks were being lit together. The clouds of fire would at times come down right to the mouth of the volcano and then suddenly burst into flames and rise a thousand feet, like a smouldering fire being showered with lac and resin. And all the while there was the sound of thousands of crackers bursting simultaneously.

The ground was shaking so violently that it was impossible to stand—they kept toppling over. Shankar somehow tottered into the tent. Inside, he noticed a small animal, very much like a puppy, that lay curled on his bed trembling with fear. Under the glare of Shankar's torch it started, but continued to look at the beam with a dazed expression, while its eyes shone like diamonds.

Alvarez entered the tent, saw it and said, 'Let it be, it has taken refuge with us out of mortal fear.'

Neither of them had seen an active fire-spewing volcano earlier. They had never imagined that this could also be a source of danger. Before Alvarez had finished speaking, they heard a tremendous noise as if something very large and heavy had dropped from a great height. Both ran outside to see what was happening. They found that a big chunk of burning rock, weighing at least fifty kilos, had crashed into a bush nearby. The bush immediately caught fire. Suddenly Alvarez was galvanised into action, and said, 'Shankar, strike tent immediately and let's run, quickly, quickly . . .'

By the time they finally folded up the tent, another half-a-dozen chunks of burning rock had crashed down around them. They could hardly breathe, the air was so heavy with smoke and sulphur fumes.

Run . . . run . . . run . . . . For two long hours they ran and somehow dragged and carried their tent and supplies—till they reached the hills on the eastern side. Even at that distance, hours later, the rain of burning rocks continued. They started climbing up the slope, through the dense forest, braving the darkness of the night. By dawn they had reached a height of about two and a half thousand feet and finally sat down to rest, panting for breath, under a large tree.

The terrible beauty of the volcano's eruption was largely subdued as the sun came up, but the noise and the rain of rocks seemed to increase. Now, together with the falling pieces of rock, a fine dust also came down from the skies. Within minutes, the trees and leaves were covered with a layer of this grey dust.

The great display of fireworks continued unabated throughout the day, till nightfall came again. In the valley below, the jungle of huge hemlock trees had been completely destroyed by the fire and the rain of rocks. At night, they saw again that terrible beauty of the volcano's eruption. The entire sky and the forests right up to the horizon were red from the fire erupting out of that huge cauldron on the mountain—only the rain of rocks had lessened a bit. But the clouds, reflecting the red-glow of the volcano, remained as fiery-red as ever.

Sometime after midnight, the sound of a tremendous explosion woke them up. With eyes full of fear they saw that the entire top of the peak had just blown off! The ash, fire and burning rocks had by then completely obliterated thc forest in the valley below. Alvarez was hit by a rock, and their tent caught fire. At the end of the show, the shower of falling rocks broke a large branch from a tree which almost fell on them!

Shankar thought—such a major natural event had taken place in this desolate forest and no one would have known about it, had they not been there. The civilised world was perhaps not even aware of the existence of this volcano in the middle of the dense jungles of Africa. People may not even believe them, if the tale were told.

In the morning, they could clearly see that the volcano's crest had developed an irregular cut at the top, like the depression made by the flame of a candle, blown by the breeze to one side of the stick. Someone had taken a second bite at the ice cream!

Alvarez studied the map and said 'The map doesn't mark it as a volcano. Probably it has become active and erupted after many years. But the name of the mountain mentioned in the map is very meaningful.'

Shankar asked, 'What's the name?' Alvarez said, 'It is written here as Oldorio Lengai—in the ancient Zulu tongue it means—the bed of the fire god. It seems from the name that the volcanic nature of the mountain was not unknown to the prehistoric people of these parts. Perhaps this volcano has been dormant for two hundred or more years.'

Shankar, the young man from India, raised both his hands, touched his forehead and saluted the mountain, Indian style, 'Accept my pranam, O Lord of Destruction! You have given me the rare privilege of witnessing your dance of destruction. O my lord, a hundred diamond mines are nothing compared to this fantastic form that you have taken. This alone is worth all my troubles and tribulations!'

Bunip

Alvarez concluded it would not be safe to journey too close to the volcanic mountain. So they left the vicinity of the peaks of the smoking, smouldering Oldorio Lengai, and travelled to the west. There was no sign of fire and carnage in the forests on the side. The vegetation had grown denser, nourished by the seasonal rain. The undergrowth was thick with bushes and small plants. The valley was full of streams, small and big, and even rivers flowing in full spate—but none of them were familiar to Alvarez.

After a while they arrived at a place surrounded by small hills of limestone and granite. Each hill was punctured by caves of varied sizes. The landscape there was a little different from the rest of the Richtersveld range. The jungles were not so dense, but the place was full of tall trees, and here and there were small hills and caves.

They camped on a small granite hillock. From the moment they arrived there, Shankar felt that the place was not a good one. There was a constant feeling of unease, an apprehension of some imminent danger—

something he didn't quite understand himself—nor could he explain this to Alvarez.

One day Alvarez said, 'Everything is wrong, Shankar. We are still roaming the same forest. Today, I noticed the same tree marked with my initials—D.A. Yet, you remember, that for the last fifteen days we have been trying to travel keeping to the west. How could we come back to the same tree again.'

Shankar said, 'Then what is the solution?'

'There is a solution. Tonight I'll have to climb to the top of a tall tree and fix our directions by looking at the stars. You stay in the tent.'

Shankar was not able to reconcile something in his mind. If they were going around in a circle, how could they have come to this place of low hills and caves? He had no recollection of having been to this part of the mountain earlier. Alvarez explained the mystery to him by saying that after he had etched his name on the tree, they didn't go any further east. If they did travel east, then another two miles would have brought them here.

That night Shankar was sitting alone in the tent and reading Bankimchandra Chattopadhyay's *Raj Singha.* This was the only book he had carried with him from Bengal and although he had read it many times, he never tired of reading it once more.

How far away was India, and in India there was Chittor, Mewar and the rivalry between the Rajputs and the Moghuls. To Shankar, wandering in the unknown forests of the unexplored continent, all that seemed as unreal as a dream.

Suddenly, he thought he heard footsteps outside the tent. At first Shankar thought Alvarez had climbed down from the tree and was coming back to the tent. But at the next instant, he knew that the footsteps were not those of a human being. If someone had tied cloth bags around his feet and then hobbled and dragged his feet along the ground—it was that kind of a sound. Alvarez's Winchester Repeater rifle was close at hand. Shankar grabbed it and sat near the tent's entrance—the rifle ready and cocked. The footsteps stopped for a while, then started again, moving along the left side of the tent. He heard the loud breathing of a large animal—just like the sounds he had heard one night travelling across the mountain—exactly the same.

Frightened out of his wits, Shankar pressed the trigger. He fired once . . . twice . . .

Within moments he heard two shots from a revolver in reply, from the top of the tree. Alvarez must have thought that Shankar must be in some kind of danger, otherwise why should he fire his revolver for nothing? He must be hurrying down from the tree.

Hearing so many guns firing, the animal must have run away—there was no sound from any side. Shankar lit his torch and came out of the tent, thinking that he would signal to Alvarez not to come down from the tree. Then suddenly he heard two more pistol shots coming from inside the jungle and immediately after that a stifled cry.

Shankar followed the sound of the pistol shots and ran into the jungle. A little distance inside, he found Alvarez lying under a tree. Looking at him in the light of the torch, Shankar trembled with fear and apprehension—his entire body was covered with blood, the head was at an impossible angle to the body, the coat was in tatters.

Shankar quickly sat down beside him and rested his head on his lap. He called—'Alvarez! Alvarez!'

There was no response from Alvarez. Once, Shankar saw his lips move, as if he wanted to say something, but there was no sound. He kept staring at Shankar, but the stare was sightless. It was an unnatural, detached, indifferent look.

Shankar carried him back to the tent and gave him water to drink. Then when he tried to take off his coat, he found that just below the neck, a chunk of flesh had been ripped out from the shoulders by some animal. The entire back was lacerated—as if some enormous, powerful beast with sharp claws or teeth had shredded the back into ribbons.

Next to where he was found, were the tell-tale marks of animal feet—feet with only three toes.

The whole night passed thus—Alvarez unresponsive, lying completely unconscious. Towards morning, Alvarez regained consciousness. He looked at Shankar with disbelieving and uncomprehending eyes—as if he had never seen him before. Then he closed his eyes again. In the afternoon he started talking, probably in his mother tongue. Shankar didn't understand a word. Late in the afternoon he suddenly looked at Shankar again. Immediately, Shankar knew that this time Alvarez had recognised him. This time he spoke in English and said, 'Shankar, what are you sitting here for? Fold up the tent, let's go.' Then, like a man senseless with drink, he lifted his hand somehow in a futile gesture of direction, and continued, 'There's a king's ransom hidden in those caves. Can't you see it? I can see it clearly. Let's go, pack up, don't delay.'

Those were Alvarez's last words.

Shankar sat in numbed silence for a long time. Evening fell, and little by little the entire forest was sunk in the depth of darkness.

Shankar suddenly woke up with a start. He quickly got up and lit a fire. Then loaded both the rifles and sat down next to Alvarez's lifeless body, keeping the guns pointed towards the tent-door.

That night, again, there was torrential rain. The force of the rainwater drilled holes in the tent and came cascading inside, drenching everything. But Shankar that night had unseeing eyes and an unfeeling body. In those few months he had really come to love Alvarez—his fearlessness, his indomitable will, his tremendous capacity for hard work—all this had fascinated Shankar. He had begun to love Alvarez like his own father. Alvarez too had developed a great fondness for him.

But more than anything else, Shankar thought of the fact that ultimately Alvarez had to die at the hands of that unknown beast, just like Jim Carter.

As the night progressed, Shankar sank increasingly into the depths of fear and despair. Somewhere close was the unknown emissary of death—and mysterious were its ways! When it would suddenly appear, and when it would go—no one knew for certain. Shankar kept fighting the tendency to doze off and sat awake the entire night.

Oh, what a terrible night it was! He would remember that night as long as he lived. The noise of rain pouring down in millions of huge drops over thousands of trees and their leaves and the howling of the wind and storm that drowned all the other sounds of the forest. From time to time he could hear the crash of trees being uprooted and felled by the storm. He was all alone in that forest on that terrifying night! The dark trunks of the trees stood like ghosts in the darkness—seen in the faint light of thousands of glow worms that were hovering around in spite of the storm.

Shankar sat in front of his friend's dead body. He must not be afraid. He must gather up courage, or he would simply die of fear. He tried concentrating on the two rifles. One was a Winchester, the other, a Mannlicher—the magazines of both were full. There was no beast made of flesh and blood that could withstand the power of those two deadly weapons and enter the tent in one piece.

Fear and danger make men brave. Shankar sat guard the whole night. The next morning, he buried Alvarez's body under a big tree and marked the grave with a cross made out of two straight branches tied together with strong creepers.

Amongst Alvarez's personal belongings, he found a diploma in mining, made out in his name, from the University of Oporto. Alvarez had passed the final examination with high honours. From their conversations, Shankar had often suspected that Alvarez was not just an uneducated fortune-hunting vagabond.

Far away from human habitation, Alvarez had at last ended his search in the depths of that desolate forest. People like him set out from home not merely in search of treasures or diamonds. Their greatest joy in life came from their obsession with danger. Such was their need to travel, intoxicated by the thrill of peril all the time, that not even the wealth of Croesus would have tied them down in one place.

Yet this was a fitting grave for the great wanderer. The trees of the forest would give cover to his last resting place! It would be haunted at night by the lion, the gorilla or the hyena. And above all, the massive Richtersveld range would stand guard at a distance forever, its head rising to the heavens, piercing the clouds above!

The Cave

That night too, passed. By then Shankar had become desperately daring. If he had to save himself from the depths of the terrible forest, he could not afford to be frightened. For two whole days he didn't move; just sat in his tent and pondered over his next move. Suddenly he remembered Alvarez saying that Salisbury was about five hundred miles to the south-east.

Salisbury! The capital of Southern Rhodesia. By whatever means, he had to reach Salisbury. He still had many years to live, it was written in his horoscope. He was not destined to die helplessly in that forest.

Shankar studied the maps as carefully as he could. A map made by the Forest Survey Department of the Portuguese government, a coastal map prepared in 1873 by the Royal Marine Survey, a map made by the famous explorer Sir Phillipo de Phillipi. Apart from these, there was a tattered old drawing made by Alvarez and signed by Jim Carter. He had made no attempts to understand or read these maps properly when Alvarez was alive. Now his life depended on his understanding of them. He had to find the shortest straight route to Salisbury. He had

check Botswana border
Due NE over again
lake with 3 streams

then to locate his own position on the map, and make his way out of the maze of the jungles of the Richtersveld—only with the help of those maps.

After a great deal of study Shankar finally came to the conclusion that none of the maps really had any specific information on those mountains and forests—except the rough drawings made by Alvarez and Jim Carter. But those were rough and written with symbols and secret codes, for both Alvarez and Carter were in constant fear that if the map fell into someone else's hands, he would demand a share of their treasure. It was almost impossible for Shankar to make sense of them.

On the fourth day, Shankar left the place where Alvarez had died and started walking eastwards as per his estimations. Before leaving, he made a garland out of wild flowers and placed it on Alvarez's resting-place.

There is an art called 'bush craft'. Without the knowledge of this art, it is extremely dangerous to try to travel across large tracts of desolate, dense and uncharted forests. Shankar had learnt a fair amount of bush craft travelling with Alvarez for so many months. But he still doubted whether he knew enough to be able to venture across that great forest all alone. He would have to depend a great deal on his destiny. If his luck held, he would succeed in crossing the forest; if luck was not in his favour, then death awaited him!

He crossed a few low hills. The jungle was sometimes dense, sometimes sparse. But everywhere there stood massive trees. Shankar did know that if he came across a jungle of elephant grass, it meant he had reached the edge of the forest because elephant grass never grew in the interior of dense forests. But here there were no signs of elephant grass—only big trees and bushes.

The first day ended in the middle of a dense forest. Shankar had left behind almost everything, except Alvarez's Mannlicher rifle, some cartridges, a water-bottle, a torch, the maps, the compass, a watch, a blanket, some medicines—and a hammock. Although the tent was fairly light, he felt it would be impossible to carry and left it behind.

He strung his hammock between two trees, quite high above the ground, and lit a fire under it to keep wild beasts away. He stretched out on the hammock with his rifle but kept awake, because sleep was impossible. On the one hand were thousands of mosquitoes, and on the other, he had noticed, since the evening, a cheetah roaming quite close to his tree. In the darkness its eyes shone like fire. The moment Shankar shone his torch on it, it would run away, but after about half-an-hour would return and stare again. Shankar was afraid that if he fell asleep, the cheetah might jump onto the hammock and attack him. Cheetahs are extremely clever animals. So Shankar could not close his eyes the whole night.

In addition, the forest was full of the sounds and cries of a variety of wild animals. At some point he had dozed off, but woke up with a start hearing the loud giggles of children. Where were the laughing children? There should not be any children either wandering around or laughing, in that uninhabited forest! The very next instant he remembered Alvarez had told him that the cries of a certain species of baboon sound just like children laughing.

In the morning he came down from his hammock and started off again. He was walking across the forest almost blindly, depending on sheer luck, in a manner which pilots would describe as 'flying blind'! He had lost all sense of direction, within just two days—he had no idea which was north and which south, which east or which west. All onc could scc wcrc trunks of trees, all around, in hundred and thousands, countless in number. Overhead was an unbroken canopy of dense foliage. The sun, moon and stars were hardly visible. During the day, very little sunlight penetrated the leafy canopy; it was like dusk all the time. Mile after mile after mile, it was the same. In any case, the compass didn't work!

On the fifth day, he stopped at the foot of a hill to rest. Nearby was the mouth of a huge cave. A thin stream came out of the cave and, winding its way, disappeared into the forest.

He had never seen such a large cave before. Overcome by curiosity, he left his baggage outside and entered the cave. There was a little light near the entrance of the cave, but further inside it was totally dark. He went carefully, torch in hand. After a while he reached a place where the cave forked into two more mouths—one to the left and one to the right. He shone his torch up and saw that the roof was very high. Thin and broad columns of calcium carbonate were hanging from it like chandeliers of solid salt!

The walls of the cave were moist, at some places water was trickling down the sides in thin streaks. Shankar entered the cave on the right. It was narrow at the mouth but widened inwards. Under his feet he felt soft earth and rocks. By the light of the torch he estimated that the cave was roughly triangular in shape. At one of the vertices of the triangle, there was another entrance. Shankar went through that and found he had entered a kind of passageway with high walls on both sides. The passage zigzagged like a snake. Shankar followed it for quite a distance.

He spent about two hours exploring the cave. Then he thought he would go back to where he had left his things. On the return journey he simply couldn't find that triangular cave. But why? The narrow cave he was in had branched out of that same triangular cave. He had come to the end of that cave—but where was the triangle?

After a frantic and fruitless search, Shankar panicked. Had he lost his way inside the cave? What a disaster!

He sat down and tried to overcome his panic by thinking clearly. No, he must not allow himself to be taken over by fear. The only way out of this danger would be through patient and clear thought. He remembered what Alvarez had told him, that when going deep into unknown places, he must mark his way so that he would be able to return by tracing those marks. He had forgotten that advice. Now, what was he to do?

He was no longer confident of using his torch all the time. If the batteries ran down, then he would be quite helpless. The cave was pitch dark. One couldn't take a step forward in that darkness, forget about finding one's way!

The whole day passed; his watch told him it was seven in the evening. The light of his torch had gradually dimmed. The inside of the cave was stifling hot and he had no drinking water with him. The water that was dripping along the walls of the cave tasted bitter and alkaline. In any case, it was a very slow drip—one had to literally lick it off the walls.

The time was seven-thirty, it must be dark outside, he thought. Time ticked on—eight, nine, ten o'clock! Shankar was still trying to grope his way around. The old batteries in the torch had been used almost continuously since three in the afternoon. The light from the torch had by then become so dim, that Shankar was almost insane with fear. He felt as if his life would last only as long as the light in the torch lasted. There was no way he would ever be able to find his way out of that darkness of hell—even Alvarez would not have succeeded.

He switched the torch off and sat in silence on a stone. He could somehow have managed to save himself if he had some light. What was he to do in that total darkness? Once he thought, let the night be over, he would make another attempt. The next instant he remembered that that would be of no help at all. Night and day were all the same inside the cave.

He started walking in the dark, groping along the wall. How sorry he felt for himself. Why hadn't he carried a couple of fresh batteries when he entered the cave? Or at least a box of matches!

His watch told him that it was morning. Not a ray of light in the perpetual darkness of the cave! Shankar was feeling exhausted and weak with hunger and thirst. Perhaps he was destined to die in the darkness of that cave. He would never see daylight again. Bloodthirsty Africa was not satisfied with the sacrifice of Alvarez. It wanted him too!

Three days and nights passed. Desperate with hunger, Shankar chewed on the inner soles of his shoes. He could not find a cockroach, a rat, or even a scorpion—anything alive that he could catch and eat. His head had started to swim, he was losing control over his conscious self—over what he was doing or going to do. The only conscious thought he had was that he had to somehow get out of that cave—he had to see daylight. So even in his exhausted, almost lifeless state, he was groping around on his hands and knees. Perhaps he would continue to do that till death overtook him.

At some point he fell asleep in his exhaustion. How long he slept he had no idea. Days, nights, hours, minutes, seconds—everything had become meaningless in that darkness. Or possibly his eyes had lost their power of vision—who knew!

He gathered a little strength after his sleep, got up and started groping his way again. He was the pupil of Alvarez. He would never let himself die by sitting and doing nothing. As long as he had life in him he would keep searching for a way out.

Strange, he thought, where was the little river? Had he lost that stream when he was roaming around that maze-like cave? If he found the river, he stood a good chance of escaping from that death-trap. Whichever way it flowed, one end of the river came out at the mouth of the cave. But for the last three days he had not even come across the smallest of streams. Shankar was about to die of thirst. His tongue had become raw and swollen, from licking the bitter, salty, foul-tasting water from the walls of the cave. His thirst, instead of being quenched, had actually increased.

Feeling the stony wall of the cave, Shankar searched for moss growing on the moist parts of the wall. At least he could survive on that. But the stone walls were completely dry; at some places, there was a thin coating of calcium carbonate. No vegetative life could survive in such total absence of sunlight.

One more day passed and night arrived. His gruelling searches had yielded nothing. He was giving up hope. How much longer should he search? It was no use, there seemed to be no end to it. Where was he going in that pitch-dark cave and through that terrifying silence! Oh, what a darkness and silence there hung in that cave! As if the world had come to an end; and in that holocaust marking the end of the universe, even the sun had been snuffed out. In that dead world's lifeless, soundless, timeless graveyard, his was the only living soul. If he stayed there much longer he would go mad.

KALAHARI

Shankar had dozed off; or perhaps he had been lying unconscious. In any case, when he woke up his watch showed twelve o'clock—most probably it was midnight. He got up and started groping again. At one point, he felt a solid rock wall in front of him—as if it was blocking his way. He flashed his dimming torch once and saw that this new rock wall blocked his path at right angles to the wall that he was following.

Suddenly he pricked up his ears because he thought he heard the faint sounds of flowing water.

Yes, it was certainly the sound of flowing water—the sound of a stream rippling across pebbles—stones breaking the flow at times. After listening carefully for some time, he felt that the sound was coming from the other side of that cave wall. He placed his ears on the cave wall and confirmed his suspicion. Searching for a break in the wall to get to the other side, he finally discovered it in the feeble light of the torch—an opening. It was a low, narrow, natural hole in the wall. He moved through it on his hands and knees for quite a distance, until he hit water. Carefully placing his hands above, he found that

the passage was high enough for him to stand. Standing up, he walked a few paces in the pitch-dark and found himself up to his ankles in ice-cold water.

Even in that darkness, he stooped down and drank that cold water to his heart's content. Then he tried to gauge the direction of the flow of the stream in the dying light of the torch. Normally the mouth of a cave is not in the upstream region of these kinds of springs. He doused his torch and tried to feel the flow of the water very carefully with his feet, and walked downstream. The stream had a winding route, sometimes running to the right, sometimes to the left. At one point he felt that it divided itself into three or four small and big streams.

When he arrived at this point he was completely confused. He shone his torch and confirmed that the stream was flowing in different directions. He remembered Alvarez's advice—if one doesn't mark one's way, then there is every possibility of getting lost.

Stooping low, he saw that on both sides of the stream there were heaps of small pebbles. The water was flowing over many of these stones.

He filled his pockets with the pebbles, and with the intention of exploring each of the streams, proceeded by placing pebbles at regular intervals on each side of the branch he was following. Having followed one stream for some distance, he found that it branched off again into smaller streams. At each junction he made an S with the pebbles.

Some of the tributaries seemed to double back towards the direction Shankar was coming from. Despite marking his way, he was getting confused.

At one place, his foot touched something cold. Lighting his torch, he saw it was a huge python coiled up in sleep. Shaken from its sleep by his touch, it looked at him with its beady eyes, but was dazzled by the beam of the torch. Otherwise, Shankar's life would have been at stake. Shankar knew that the python was a dangerous reptile—one may be able to escape from the clutches of a tiger or lion—but it was impossible to get out of the coils of a python. If once the snake had coiled its tail round his feet, he was finished.

Now he was really terrified of walking in that darkness. Who knows where another python may be lurking coiled up! After following two or three branch streams for a while he returned to his starting position with the help of his pebble markings. At the main junction of the streams, he had made the mark of a cross. He then tried to follow one of them, guessing it was the main stream. Even this one didn't flow straight. After some distance it too divided itself into several smaller streams. At places, the roof of the cave hung so low that he had to walk bent double like an eighty-year-old.

Suddenly, at one place, he shone his torch, and even in its dim light, he could make out that the cave was triangular there. That same triangular cave, which he had lost and because of which he almost reached the doorsteps of death! A little later, he saw, far in the distance, a few stars framed by the darkness. He had arrived at the cave mouth! No more fear. He had managed to save himself.

When Shankar finally came out into the open, it was three in the morning. The trees were a little scattered in that place and he could see the star-studded sky above. Coming out of that terrible darkness, the clear star-lit sky seemed to him like the brightly lit streets of a big city! He thanked God with all his heart for the entirely unexpected escape he had made.

Dawn arrived. The early rays of the sun hit the tops of the branches of trees and lit them up like hundreds of bright lights; Shankar decided he would not spend a moment more in that inauspicious place. He still had one of the pebbles from the cave in his pocket. Instead of throwing it away, he kept it as a reminder of the perils of the cave.

The next day he came across elephant grass in the forest. The jungle gave way to open land that same evening. At night, Shankar studied the map very carefully. The grassland country that he could now see stretched for almost three hundred miles right up to the Zambesi river. Over a major part of that distance stretched the famous Kalahari desert. For approximately 175 miles, there would be terrifying, desolate, waterless, trackless desert land. From military maps, Alvarez had figured out and noted that the only sensible route would be to follow a particular north-easterly track. Any attempt to cut through the middle would be inviting death. In the map, the area was marked—The Land of Thirst! If he could somehow manage to reach Rhodesia, the journey would become much easier, because those were inhabited areas.

Shankar then displayed exemplary courage. In spite of realising the dangers of the impending journey, he did not lose heart or become numb with fear. Alvarez had said he would go alone, down that route to Salisbury, to buy food and cartridges. How could he back away from something that a sixty-two year old man was resolved to do?

But courage and daring is one thing; knowledge and experience quite another! Shankar had never learnt how to fix the direction of his destination by reading a map. He found he didn't really understand the maps at all. The military maps, instead of marking the two oases in the desert, indicated only the latitudes and longitudes. There were some very complicated calculations to gauge the 'true north' from the 'magnetic north' which Alvarez used to do. But Shankar had never bothered to learn those calculations.

Hence, he had no option but to depend on fate. He decided to try and cross that huge difficult stretch of desert, depending entirely on his luck and destiny. As a result, in hardly two days, he was completely lost. Any experienced traveller would have found the oasis blind-folded, after studying the maps. But Shankar missed it by three miles. He had almost finished the water he was carrying. If he did not find water soon, he would die.

First, he had to encounter the vast expanse of open dry-land and hills, full of cactus and euphorbia shrubs, interspersed with mounds of granite. Then there was the excruciatingly painful and difficult journey! No food, no water, no sense of direction, no human face to see. Day after day of mindless, fruitless trudging, looking only at the horizon, with no hope. From the skies the sun blazed down like hell-fire, and below his feet was sand, hot as burning coal. The sun rose and set, the stars appeared, the moon came up—and went down—countless times. In the evening and even late at night, all he could hear were the monotonous calls of the lizards or the chirping of crickets.

There were no milestones, no count of the miles he had travelled. Food was a stray bird, or at times the flesh of a buzzard—the vulture of the desert—whose meat was tough and foul-tasting. There were days when the pangs of hunger were such that even a poisonous scorpion, whose sting could kill, was considered a tasty meal and a fortunate find.

After two days of intense thirst, he found a little pool of water in a crevice on a hill. The colour of the water was red, strange insects were floating on the surface and the bloated carcass of some dead animal was lying on its bank. Yet Shankar drank his fill of that water and saved himself.

Day followed day, months passed, Shankar had no count of weeks or years. He had become thin and emaciated. He didn't know where he was going—all he knew was that he had to press on. India and Bengal lay ahead of him.

Then he arrived in the real Kalahari desert. Shankar trembled with fear even looking at it from a distance. How could any man cross this burning expanse of sand? All one could see were sand dunes and a sea of burnt coppery sand. In the afternoon sun, the landscape appeared to be on fire. At the edge of the desert, his thermometer showed a temperature of 127 degrees even in the shade.

It was emphatically indicated on the map that it was impossible to cross the desert, except by following the north-east track. Any attempt to cross it by cutting across the centre would mean inevitable death, because there was no water on the entire route. It was not as if there was plenty of water on the north-eastern side either; but at distances of thirty, seventy, and ninety miles, there were three natural springs. But these springs were hidden in the cracks and crevices of the hills, and were very difficult to find. This was the reason why the latitudes and longitudes were so well marked in the military maps.

Shankar thought he would never be able to work out the calculations and find those springs. He had a sextant and a chart indicating the positions of stars—but he didn't know how to use them. Whatever had to happen would happen—he was in God's hands. But he would try his best to proceed, keeping to the north-east.

On the third day, by sheer providence, he came across a small spring. The water was muddy and boiling hot—but even that was as rare and welcome as nectar. The desert became more and more fierce. All signs of animal or vegetable life gradually vanished. Earlier Shankar's fire at night would attract a few insects; now they too were no longer to be found.

The days were as hot as the nights were cold. Towards morning the temperature dropped so low that his hands and feet almost froze. And gradually his means of lighting a fire were also gone. There was no firewood to be found anywhere. In a few days, the water that he carried was also finished. In that vast sea of sand, it was easier to find a familiar speck of sand, than to find those small springs which were hardly a yard across in width.

One evening Shankar almost went mad with thirst. He had realised by then, that his attempt to cross that terrible desert on his own even keeping to the north-east, was as good as committing suicide. Yet he had come so far; there was no question of going back.

He climbed a fairly high dune to survey the area. He found only dunes around him, except that the ones to the east seemed higher. Although the sun had set, the entire sky was still red. At some distance from him, there was a small hillock and he thought he could see a cave in that hill. These granite hillocks were to be found throughout that region. In Transvaal and Rhodesia they were known as 'kopje' or small hill. At night, Shankar took shelter in that cave to escape from the cold.

Something quite remarkable happened there.

ATTILEO'S GIFT

On entering the cave Shankar shone his torch (now freshly loaded with new batteries) and found that it was quite small. It was the size of a small room, and the floor was strewn with countless small stones. Then his eyes fell on a wooden cask in one corner of the cave. Now, how did that wooden cask get there?

A couple of steps ahead, he got a shock!

Lying against the wall of the cave was a human skeleton, white with age. The skull was turned towards the wall. Around the skeleton were bits of black fabric, perhaps the remains of a woollen coat. A pair of boots were still strapped to the feet. On one side was a rusted gun.

Next to the wooden cask was a bottle, closed with a cork. Inside the bottle were some pieces of paper. Shankar uncorked the bottle, took out the paper and saw something written in English.

He was curious to see what was in the cask. But the moment he tried to shift it, there was a loud hissing sound which froze his blood! In an instant a huge snake

nothing compared to that
mine. My life is about
to end, but what to do?
What a terrible desert!
Not even the chirping of
a cricket anywhere. &
keep reminding myself &
never set my eyes
again on the beautiful

leapt up at least a yard and a half from the ground. The snake must have missed him by a second, and that single second saved Shankar's life. In the next instant, his automatic Colt 45 roared to life. In a moment, the head of that huge sand viper was shattered to bits, its blood and flesh splattered all over—on the cask, on the walls and on the floor. Alvarez had taught him to keep himself ready all the time. That advice had saved his life over and over again.

What an escape! He examined the cask and saw that there was some water left in it. It was black like ink, but it was still water. He lifted the small cask and drank that foul-smelling inky water, to his fill. Then he examined the body of the snake with the help of his torch. The snake was about ten feet long and quite thick. These snakes hide their bodies in the sand—keeping only their heads exposed—they are deadly.

Then he put together the bits of paper he had recovered from the bottle and began to read. He even found the small pencil that was used to write the message, inside the bottle.

Attileo's Message

'I am about to die. Tonight is probably my last. After my death, if someone attempting to cross this terrible desert takes shelter in this cave, he may find this piece of paper.

My donkey died in the desert two days ago. It was carrying a cask of water. I brought that cask back and put it here in this cave, in spite of the fact that I am weak with fever. I don't even have the strength to get up. In any case, I am already exhausted by hunger.

My name is Attileo Gatti and I'm twenty-six years old. I was born in the Gatti family of Florence. The famous navigator Rioleno Cavalcanti Gatti, who fought in the Battle of Lepanto against the Turks, was one of my forefathers.

I studied at the universities of Rome and Pisa. But the lure of the sea kindled in me a desire to travel—historically the addiction of the Gatti family. On one expedition—a voyage to the Dutch East Indies—our ship sank on the coast of West Africa. Only seven of us managed to reach the shore somehow. West Africa has many dense forests. In one forest, we took refuge in a village of the Shefu tribe. We stayed there for almost two months. There, by chance, we heard tales of a huge diamond mine. We were told that the diamond mine was located somewhere towards the east, inside a massive range full of impenetrable forests.

The seven of us decided that we must somehow find the diamond mine. I was elected the leader of the group. We set out for that unknown mountain, cutting through dense forests. None of the villagers would come with us to show us the way. They said that they had never been there and did not know where it was. They told us that the forest was guarded by a jungle god, and that no one succeeded in bringing back any diamonds from there.

But we were not to be discouraged. On the way, two of our companions died from the terrible torture of the journey. The other four refused to go any further. I was the leader, born in the Gatti family. I would never go back. All I know is that as long as there is life in the body, one has to go forward. I did not want to return.

My body is giving up. The emissary of death will visit me tonight. How beautiful is our little Selino Lagrano. On its banks stands our ancestral palace—Castelli Riolini. Even from this distance, I can smell the fragrance of the lemon flowers, from the lemon orchard on the shores of the Selino Lagrano. I can hear the sweet peal of the silver bells of the little church at the foot of the hill.

No, what nonsense am I writing in my feverish stupor! Let me say what I really want to. I cannot write for much longer!

We crossed the mountains and the forest. We found the diamond mine. The source of the river, where the diamonds can be found, is in a huge and terrifying cave. I entered that cave and saw that the banks and bed of the river were strewn with countless diamonds. Every stone was a tetrahedron crystal, clear and yellowish. There are no diamonds like those in the markets of London and Amsterdam.

I have seen the jungle god of those forests and mountains—from a distance, like a shadowy figure, in the light of a torch. He didn't come near me because I held that burning light in my hand. He probably lives in that cave. That is perhaps the reason why the legend says that he is the guardian of the diamond mine.

But finding the mine turned into a curse for me: and even worse was my decision to talk about it to my companions. When I entered the cave a second time, taking my friends with me, I could not find the mine. It was pitch dark inside, the light from burning fire-wood torches were hardly sufficient. On top of that, the river broke into so many branches, that it was impossible to single out the stream that flowed over the diamonds.

My companions were uncouth, uncivilised sailors. They thought I was pretending to have lost the diamond mine so as to deprive them. They thought I wanted to take it all for myself. What conspiracy they hatched between them I don't know, but the next evening the four of them suddenly attacked me with knives. But they didn't know what Attileo Gatti was made of. The warm blood that flowed in my veins was that of my forefather Rioleno Cavalcanti Gatti, who sent many such savages to hell.

When I was a cadet in the military academy at Santa Calina, I could wound even the best fencer of the region, Antonid Dryfus, in a duel with knives. Two of the brutes died fighting me; the other two were mortally wounded and died the same night. I thought that I would not be able to find the diamond mine, in the maze of that dark cave. And I was seriously wounded! I had to reach the civilised world. I started off towards the east, hoping to reach the Dutch Colonies. But I was not able to go any further than this. They knifed me in the lower abdomen. That wound became septic, and together with that came the fever. I wondered at how greedy men can be. Why did they attack me? They were my companions. I had not once thought of depriving or cheating them!

I am the owner of the world's greatest diamond mine, because I risked my very life to discover it. The person reading this letter will certainly be a civilised person and a Christian. It is my earnest request to him that he give me a proper Christian burial. In return, I bestow upon him the rights to my diamond mine!

My life is about to end, but what can I do?? What a terrible desert this is! Not even the chirping of a cricket can be heard anywhere. What strange places exist in this world. I kept telling myself today that I'll never again see the beautiful Selino Lagrano lake surrounded by poplars. Nor will I ever look upon the fourteenth century church next to the lake and hear the blessed peals of its large silver bell. I can see our old palace on the hill—Castelli Riolini, looking like a monarch's castle—In the distance I can see the green fields of Umbria and the little river flowing through vineyards—sorry, I am raving again.

Sitting at the cave door I am looking at the countless stars in the sky, to my heart's content—for the last time. I remember St. Franco's hymn to the sun.

Another thing. Five large diamonds are hidden in my boots. I give them to you, my unknown traveller friend. Please do not forget my last request. May Mother Mary bless you.

Commander Attileo Gatti
1880 A.D. (probably the month of March)

What an ill-fated young man!

Thirty long years had gone by since his death. No one passed that way since he died—no one had entered the cave. After such a long time, the letter finally fell into human hands.

How amazing, that even after thirty years, the wooden cask still had water in it.

As soon as he had read the letter, Shankar knew that it was the same cave that Attileo had described—the cave where he had lost his way and almost died. Then, out of curiosity, he pulled the boots from the skeletal feet, and five large diamonds fell out. They looked exactly like the pebbles he had filled his pockets with, to mark his way in the dark cave. He still had one like that, in his pocket. He had seen heaps and heaps of them on the river bed under the flowing waters and along the banks. Who knew then—that the diamond mine for which he and Alvarez were searching, having come all the way from across the seven seas and many more rivers, completely frustrated and exhausted, roaming in the wilds of the Richtersveld—was to be found in that totally unexpected manner! Who would ever think that diamonds could be lying around in innumerable heaps, like ordinary pebbles! If he had known he would have filled his pockets with them.

But he had made a terrible mistake. He had not prepared any map or even a sketch of the location of that cave in which the treasure lay. Nor did he leave any marks or signs, by which he could find it again. In that huge, mountainous, forested region, he had no idea where he had come across that cave by sheer chance. He would probably not be able to find it again in future. But he had been grievously wounded soon after he discovered the diamond mine, and it was natural for him to make that mistake. Perhaps, he could have made his way back—but surely that was beyond Shankar's capacity now.

Suddenly he remembered Alvarez' dying words, 'Shankar, let's go. There's a king's treasure hidden in that cave. Can't you see it? I can see it clearly.'

Shankar buried the skeleton in the cave. He broke the cask, and made a crude cross out of two planks, fixing them with the rusted nails. Then he marked the grave with the cross. He didn't know much more about a proper Christian burial. He then prayed to God, asking him to bless the soul of the unfortunate young man.

Doing all that took the whole day. He rested that night and set off again the next morning, taking with him the letter and the diamonds.

He was convinced that whoever went in search of the cursed diamond mine, never returned to civilisation. Attileo Gatti and his companions died, Jim Carter died, Alvarez died. How many people had died before them, who knew? Now it was his turn. He would meet his end in that desert, just like the brave young Italian man.

The Final Stretch

When the afternoon sun set fire to everything around, Shankar took shelter in the shadow of a small mound. His thermometer showed 135 degrees! No man of flesh and blood could walk through that heat. If he could somehow escape its deadly clutches, he had some chance of reaching human habitation, alive. He knew that parts of the Kalahari Desert were also the abode of lions. He had a rifle with him—even in the middle of the night, he was not afraid of facing a lion all alone. But his real fear was thirst—that terrible demon.

Twice, in the afternoon, he saw mirages. Even on this long trek across the desert, he had not encountered this fascinating natural phenomenon until then. He had read about it only in books. One mirage appeared in the north-east and another one in the opposite direction. Both of them produced almost identical pictures—either a mosque or a church with a large dome, date-palm trees all around and a large lake in front. The mirage in the north-east appeared more vivid.

Towards the evening, he saw a mountain range in the distance, like clouds on the horizon. Shankar could not

believe his eyes! There was only one mountain range to his east, from which it would be possible to see the Chimanimani mountains on the borders of southern Rhodesia. Did that mean that he had almost crossed the great Kalahari on foot? Or was that a mirage too?

But at ten o'clock on the same night, he could see the outlines of the range, just as clearly. No one had ever seen a mirage in moonlight or starlight. Then it was not one! A million thanks to God!

Was there then hope for his life? Today, he was the owner of the largest diamond mine in the world. He had earned that right with his superhuman toils and extreme courage. If only he could return to his country, his poor Bengal, alive.

At the end of two days, he reached the foot of the mountain. Then he realised that there was no way across, except by climbing the mountain. Otherwise, he would have to take a detour of twenty-five miles across the desert and go around the southern edge of the mountain. He was in no mood to enter the desert again. He would rather cross the mountain!

Here, he made a major mistake. He forgot that it was no easy task to scale a mountain that was twelve and a half thousand feet high. It was as difficult as crossing the Richtersveld. Actually it would be even worse—because in the Richtersveld, Alvarez was with him; here he was alone.

Shankar failed to comprehend the perils involved in his decision. As a result, he nearly lost his life in his attempt to traverse the Chimanimani mountains. Even in the terrible fire-like Kalahari, he did not have to face such certain death.

The jungles of the Chimanimani mountains were not very dense. Shankar climbed quite high on the first day. Then he landed himself in a place from where it was not possible to move in any direction. He couldn't even retrace the way he had come up. He felt that he had deviated at least thirty degrees to the south from the place in the plains where he had started his climb. He couldn't understand why or how it had happened. He was fixing his direction by looking at the sun, and yet why was he taking so many days to cross the seven or eight miles of the width of the range?

On the third day, he faced a new kind of problem. The day before, a loose rock had rolled down and hit his leg. He hadn't felt too much pain at that time. But the next day he could hardly get up. His knee was swollen and the leg hurt terribly. In such a condition, it was impossible to negotiate mountain terrain. He had managed to collect some spring water while he was climbing up. He would have to stay at that place, until his leg got better, or at least hurt less. He would not go far, but would at least be able to find some food and water. Luckily, that particular spot on the mountain was fairly flat.

In such situations, danger lurked at every step. Any European explorer would have faced similar problems, had he tried to cross the mountain alone.

Shankar was at the end of his tether. Now, even a little walking would send his heart palpitating and go thump-thump against his ribs. The terrible exertions of his journey, constant worries and anxieties, inedible food and bouts of near-starvation had completely ruined his health.

On the fourth day, in a state of total exhaustion, he took shelter under a tree. He had not eaten since the previous day. He had his rifle with him, but there was no sign of any wild animal. In the afternoon, a deer grazing nearby had brought some hope. But his rifle was resting against a tree, fifty yards away! By the time he could get to it, the deer ran away. There was very little water left in the leather pouch. How was he to go down and get water from the spring in that condition? The swelling had increased and the pain was so excruciating, that even the slightest movement would almost blow his head off with agony.

Under the clear sky one could see up to long distances quite clearly. Far ahead, the blue mountains covered the entire horizon. The great Kalahari stretched all the way to the south-west horizon. To the south were the Wahkuhock mountains. Far behind that, like distant clouds, one could see the Krueger mountains. Shankar could not see Salisbury though. The high peaks of the Chimanimani range blocked the view.

Vultures began to circle above him. Fear had never really completely gripped Shankar in all his travels, as it did at the sight of the vultures. The birds sensed that they would not have to wait long for their prey.

A little after dusk, he heard a sound, looked around and spotted a grey wolf behind a rock. The long pointed ears of the wolf pricked up, and he saw its red tongue hanging out from between rows of white teeth. As soon as Shankar's eyes met the wolf's, the beast quickly disappeared behind the rock and ran away.

Had the wolf also come to know that his end was near? They say that animals have a sixth sense and can sense things before they happen.

The night was bone-chilling cold. Shankar lit a fire with the few twigs and branches he could gather. Apart from the faint light of the fire, it was pitch dark all around.

An animal quietly lay down, blending with the darkness, at a little distance. It was a coyote—an animal related to the dog family. A little while later, it was joined by another one, then another two, then three. . . . As the night progressed, at least twelve or fifteen had gathered. They seemed to be waiting for something to happen, sitting all around him in that darkness.

What ominous signs!

His blood ran cold in his veins. It was true then, that his days were coming to an end. He too had failed in his attempt to escape with the diamonds of the Richtersveld!

Oh! How fabulously wealthy he was today. Forget the diamond mine, even the six diamonds he had with him would be worth at least two or three lakh rupees. If only he could reach his poor village and the humble home of his parents with that money! How many tears of poverty he could wipe off; how many poor unmarried girls he could find good husbands for, and with handsome dowries; how many old men and women in their last few days he could ensure carefree lives for!

But what was the point of dreaming about things that were never to happen? Better to enjoy the beauty of the night, made more beautiful by the light of the stars above; the deep silent night of the mountains and forests. Before he died, he too would fill his eyes and his heart with beauty just like the young Italian—Gatti. They were all strung together by the same thread of fate—Attileo Gatti and his companions, Jim Carter, Alvarez and Shankar!

As the night progressed, it became increasingly cold. He looked out into the darkness and saw that the pack of coyotes had come closer. Their eyes shone bright in the light thrown by the flames of the fire. Shankar threw a burning log at them and they ran away. But how silent their movements were, and what infinite patience they had! Shankar felt they knew that their prey was within their reach; there was no way they would let it go.

In the meanwhile, the grey wolf had come around at least twice, lurking behind the coyotes.

Shankar dared not go to sleep. Who knows, perhaps the coyotes and the wolf would start tearing at him alive, taking him for dead. Although tired and exhausted, he must keep sitting fully awake. From time to time, the coyotes would come near and then run away, as he pelted them with burning logs. By that time, a couple of hyenas had joined the throng. How their eyes shone in the darkness!

What a terrible situation. He was sitting all alone on a bleak mountain top, three and a half thousand feet high, in the midst of a savage and desolate country, completely immobile, in the dead of the night, with only a fire in front of him to give him comfort. Above him, countless stars shone in the sky, like electric bulbs, their light intensified by the still atmosphere. And below that, in the darkness, lurked packs of wolves, coyotes and hyenas, lusting for his flesh.

At the same time he thought, at least he was not panting for breath, stricken with malaria in his village in Bengal. This death would be a courageous death. He had crossed the Kalahari by foot, all alone. His name would be etched in the rocks of the Chimanimani mountains after his death. He was a distinguished traveller and explorer. He had discovered that enormous diamond mine. After Alvarez met his death, he had negotiated the Richtersveld mountains and its maze of forests, all alone, and was able to survive this far. But now he was helpless, unable to move. Yet he was fighting still; he had not forsaken his courage. Life and death were in the hands of providence. If he didn't live, it was not his fault.

The long night ended at last, and the eastern sky was alight. The wild beasts vanished. The day progressed, the sun came up and started roasting the countryside in all directions. And out of nowhere, the vultures reappeared. Some circled above, some perched on rocks, on the branches of trees, and waited patiently. They seemed to say, 'Where will you go my pet? Jump around as long as you can. We are in no hurry, we'll wait.'

Shankar had lost his appetite. In spite of that, he shot and killed a vulture. The sun was blazing hot, it was impossible to step on the hot rocks. He retrieved the dead vulture, and lighting a fire, started roasting it. Earlier he had eaten vulture flesh in the desert. They were the only means to keep body and soul together there. Today he was eating them, tomorrow they would eat him! The vultures had begun circling above him again.

His shadow had fallen on the rocks. In that desolate spot, Shankar's agitated and confused mind found a companion even in that shadow. Perhaps he was going mad! In his delirium, he found himself talking to his own shadow many times. He had to make a conscious effort to stop himself.

Was he really going crazy? Did he have a fever? Everything was confusing. Alvarez . . . diamond mine . . . mountains, hills, seas of sand . . . Attileo Gatti . . . he couldn't sleep last night . . . another night was coming, he would sleep then.

Shankar had dozed off, when a strange sound woke him up. From where? It was not a familiar sound. What was it? He couldn't make out the direction from which the sound was coming. But suddenly it was approaching him.

Suddenly Shankar happened to look up at the sky and he stared in great astonishment. Something was flying across the sky above him, making a terrific noise. Was that an aeroplane? He had seen pictures of aeroplanes in books.

When the aircraft was just above him, Shankar shouted and waved broken branches, but couldn't attract the attention of the pilot. Within minutes the aeroplane disappeared behind the violet-coloured peaks of the Krueger mountains.

Perhaps more aeroplanes would pass that way. What a wonderful sight the aeroplane was. He had never seen one in India.

Shankar thought he would light a fire, so that the smoke would catch the pilot's attention if the aeroplane went back that way. At least all the vultures had disappeared, terrified by the tremendous noise of the aircraft.

The day passed. As the daylight faded and night returned, Shankar's problems began again. The coyotes returned. They spread themselves out around the fire. No sooner than it was dusk, the wolf came and took a good look at him from a distance. Then it came back again late at night.

How could he get rid of them? He couldn't afford to fire his gun to scare them off. He had only two cartridges left. If he ran out of bullets, he would have to die of starvation. Die he would of course, sooner or later. But he would hope for as long as he breathed.

But ultimately he was forced to fire. Late at night, the hyenas came, and with their support, the coyotes became bolder. They came forward and began to surround him. They could no longer be frightened by burning logs. At some point he dozed off and kept falling down from his sitting position. Then suddenly he woke up and found that the wolf had been silently approaching and had come very close to him. Out of sheer fright, he fired his gun.

The coyotes had infinite patience. They kept waiting, silently. But the wolf was looking for an opportunity.

As soon as it was morning, the coyotes, the hyenas and the wolf disappeared like a bad dream. Shankar immediately lay down near the fire and fell asleep.

Some kind of sound woke him up. It was loud. The echo was still ringing in Shankar's ears.

Was someone firing a gun? Impossible. Who would come into these impassable mountains?

He had only one bullet left. Placing his faith entirely on providence, he fired the last shot. Whatever lay in store for him could not be worse than death. He heard two shots in reply.

In his joy and excitement, Shankar forgot that one of his legs could not possibly take him very far. He had no cartridges left, so he couldn't fire his gun anymore; instead he shouted as loudly as he could. He broke branches and waved them frantically, looking around for twigs and dry wood to light a fire.

A party surveying the Krueger National Park was travelling from Kimberly to Cape Town. On the way they had camped at the foot of the Chimanimani mountains, at the north-east corner of the Kalahari Desert. They were travelling in seven large caterpillar-belted motorised vehicles, and consisted of nine Europeans and a number of black coolies. Four of them had climbed up the lower ranges of the Chimanimani, to hunt for deer.

They were extremely surprised to hear the sound of a rifle shot in that desolate forest. When they didn't receive a reply to their own signal, they started searching. They climbed to a slightly higher point, and saw from there, a strange, skeletal, ghost-like creature, with sunken eyes and an emaciated face, trying to draw their attention with screams and gestures. He was wearing a dirty and tattered European dress.

They ran to him. They couldn't understand a word of Shankar's incoherent babble. They carefully lifted him and carried him to their camp. They recovered his meagre belongings and laid him down to sleep.

But Shankar had to suffer quite a bit. Prolonged hunger, the wound in his leg, physical exhaustion, constant anxiety and poor food had completely ruined his health. He had high fever that night. He had lost consciousness in his delirium, and had no idea when they started from the camp and when they reached Salisbury. He had to spend fifteen days in a Salisbury hospital in that condition. Then, he took almost another month to get slightly better. When he was discharged from the hospital, he came out and stood on the main street of Salisbury.

Blue Sea

Salisbury! How long had he dreamed of Salisbury!

Today, he was really standing on the pavement of a large city. Big buildings, banks, hotels, shops; and a well-paved broad road, with electric trams running on one side. Zulu rickshaw-pullers were pulling rickshaws, the newspaper man was selling newspapers. All these scenes seemed new and strange to him, as if he had never seen such sights before.

He had returned to civilisation. But without a penny in his pocket. He didn't even have money to buy a cup of tea. He spotted an Indian shop and felt very happy. How long had it been since he had seen the face of an Indian? The shopkeeper was a Memon Muslim, and he was selling soaps and groceries wholesale. It was a very large shop. One look at Shankar, and he knew that the young man was poor and in some difficulty. He gave him two rupees, and asked him to go and see another rich Indian trader in town.

Before leaving with the two rupees in his pocket, Shankar told the shopkeeper 'Many many thanks for your kind help with these two rupees. But please consider

BANK
Mithila H.

this a loan. You must take this back, as soon as I have a little money with me.'

Nearby was an Indian restaurant. He could not resist the temptation to eat some good food. How long it had been since he had tasted civilised food! He went in and spent a rupee and had his fill of puris, kachoris, mutton cutlets and cake, and washed all that down with two or three cups of tea.

While eating in the restaurant he noticed an old newspaper lying on the table. One of the news items had a bold headline, saying:

STRANGE EXPERIENCE OF THE NATIONAL SURVEY TEAM

Discovery of a Dying and Exhausted Indian in the Desert: His Amazing Story

Shankar saw that there was even a painted picture accompanying the news item. The story that followed the headlines was completely fabricated. He had never told anyone such a story.

The newspaper was called the *Salisbury Daily Chronicle*. Shankar found his way to the newspaper office and identified himself. A crowd soon gathered around him. He learnt that the reporters had tried very hard to find him. He was given fifty rupees for his story of being stranded on the Chimanimani mountains with a broken leg, and for his photograph. From that sum, he first returned the loan of two rupees to the kind-hearted Muslim gentleman.

He wrote an article for the newspaper about the volcano. He named the volcano—Mount Alvarez—in his article. But only some people believed that such a huge active volcano could be hidden for so long in the jungles of Central Africa—others were skeptical. Of course, he was careful that not even a wisp of information about the diamond mine escaped his mouth. If it did, there would be a mad rush of people searching for the mine.

He then found a bookshop and bought a big bundle of books and magazines in English. How long it had been since he had read a book! In the evening he saw a picture in a movie-hall. After ages, he was lying on a proper and comfortable bed in a hotel and reading a book under the glare of an electric bulb. From time to time, he looked out of the window and gazed down at the traffic flowing through Prince Albert Victor Street. There were trams, rickshaws, little bells rang from the Indian coffee shop, even a few motor cars could be seen passing. Then he imagined another picture—a log-fire in front; a little further away packs of coyotes and hyenas were sitting all around in a circle; and behind them the two round eyes of the wolf were burning like red-hot embers.

Which one was the dream? That terrifying night in the Chimanimani mountains, or this present night?

Meanwhile, Shankar had become quite a celebrity in Salisbury. His hotel was always full of reporters. Representatives of newspapers and magazines came, asking him to sign contracts for publishing accounts of his travels or for taking his photograph.

He went to the Italian Consul General, and narrated the story of Attileo Gatti. Looking through old records in their office, it came to light that a young man from an aristocratic Italian family—called Attileo Gatti—landed on the coast of Portuguese West Africa after his ship was wrecked on that coast in 1879. No trace of the young man could be found after that. His relatives were rich and well-known people. They searched for him continuously from 1890 to 1895 and during these years had made life miserable for the people in the consulate offices of East, West, and South Africa. They had even declared a handsome prize for anyone who had information about him. They finally gave up in 1895.

With the help of his friend the Muslim shopkeeper, Shankar was able to sell four of his diamonds to Messrs Rydall and Morseby, one of the biggest jewellers on Blackmoon Street, for Rs. 32,500. The price for the other two were quoted much higher, but Shankar wanted to take them home to show his mother. He didn't wish to sell them here.

Blue Sea!

Standing on the deck of his Bombay-bound ship leaving the port of Beira in Portuguese East Africa, Shankar was gazing out at the slowly disappearing coast with its green coconut palm trees and wondering about his adventures. This was life, this was how he had always wanted to live his life. A man's age was the wrong measure of a man's life. In those eighteen months, he had gained the experience of ten years. Today he was not merely an intrepid traveller, he was the co-discoverer of an active volcano. He would make Mount Alvarez a famous landmark.

But now his heart was anxious to return to his sacred motherland, waiting across the Indian Ocean. He was impatient to set his eyes on the famous Rajabhai Towers of Bombay, from a distance, so that he would know he had finally arrived. Then later he would reach his tiny village at the edge of Bengal, reverberating with the music of baul and kirtan. Spring was on its way, the village paths would be strewn with flowers from the safina tree, the nightingale would sing from the branches of their bokul tree, and at last the country-boat carrying him would arrive at the little jetty on the river.

'Goodbye, Alvarez my friend. In this moment of happiness, on my way back home to my country, I am filled with thoughts of you. You are one of those few, whose roof is the entire sky, and the entire world your arena. Bless me from your quiet resting-place in the great

African jungle, so that I too can follow your example, and remain unaffected by happiness or misery and be as brave in life.

Goodbye to you too, Attileo Gatti. You must have been my friend in a previous life.

Both of you together taught me the truth of that ancient Chinese saying—Instead of the fixed, immovable and undisturbed life of a tile on a flat terrace, it is far better to be even a broken piece of crystal; far, far better.'

He would go back to Africa. But now he must answer the call of the motherland. He would spend some time in his country. Then he would try and form a company, and return to the far-away Richtersveld mountains to search for the diamond mine. He was determined to find it.

Appendix

While in Salisbury, Shankar had gone and met Dr Fitzgerald, the famous biologist and curator of the South Rhodesian Museum, to ask him about the Bunip. Sometime after he had returned to India, he received the following letter from him:

January 11, 1911

The South Rhodesian Museum
Salisbury, Rhodesia
South Africa.

Dear Mr Choudhuri,

I am writing this letter to fulfil my promise to you, to let you know what I thought about your report of a strange three-toed monster in the wilds of the Richtersveld mountains. While looking through my files I found some similar accounts by explorers who had been to the region before you. There is one in particular by Sir Robert McCulloch, the famous naturalist, whose report has not yet been published, owing to his sudden and untimely death last year.

On thinking the matter over, I am inclined to believe that the monster you saw was none other than one of a species of the anthropoid ape, closely related to the gorilla, but much bigger and more savage than those found in the Ruwenzori and Virunga mountains. This species is becoming more and more rare every day; and such numbers of those that do exist are not easy to ascertain on account of their shyness, and because they hide in the depths of the high-altitude rain forests of the Richtersveld. It is only a very fortunate traveller that has a glimpse of them, and I should think that in meeting them he runs a risk proportionate to his good fortune.

Congratulating you on both your luck and pluck,

I remain,

Yours sincerely
J. G. Fitzgerald

Glossary

Ashwathwa	the Banyan or the Indian fig tree
Barah Bhuyians	the twelve kings of Bengal
Bunip	variation of Bunyip, a fabulous monster of swamps and lagoons (in Australian aboriginal myths)
Chapatis	a small flat thin cake of unleavened bread (in Indian cuisine)
Kaffir	member of one of the Bantu-speaking tribes of South Africa (usage now obsolete)
Matabele	now called the Ndebele, members of a Bantu-speaking people living mainly in Zimbabwe and Transvaal
Okapi	a rare mammal of the giraffe family, native to the Congolese rain-forest
Safina	the drumstick tree
Saptarisi-mandal	a constellation of seven stars, also known as Ursa Major or the Big Dipper

Simba	lion (in the Masai tongue)
Sola hat	sun-hat
Veldt	open grassland
Yama	god of death in Hindu mythology
Yuca tree	an arborescent species of the agave family of plants